ABOUT FACE:

A Redirection in Education

ABOUT FACE:
A Redirection in Education

How both sons of a single mother
were homeschooled and admitted
to college by the time they were twelve

By
EVA SEIBERT

Foreword by Dr. Robert J. Pushaw

Published by:
Eva Seibert
P.O. Box 1293
Raymore, MO 64083
(816) 318-1110

Printed in the United States

ISBN: 1-890622-37-0

Library of Congress Catalog Card No. 98-066616

To my mother, Marion Kuhns,
who read *The Boxcar Children* to me.

ACKNOWLEDGMENTS

I am grateful to many people who supported my efforts in homeschooling. I am grateful to the following people who helped me with this book.

Bill Silcox, Hilary Weeks and Norma King for proofreading, advising, and sharing their ideas.

Professor Robert Pushaw for teaching my son in law school and for adding to my confidence.

Jim and Julie Link for being such good people.

My sons Russell Boyd and Robert Boyd for being so patient when things seemed unorganized.

My husband Rich for loving me and encouraging me to see this project through.

TABLE OF CONTENTS

FOREWORD

As a professor at the University of Missouri School of Law who believes that life experience is invaluable to understanding the law, I was highly skeptical when I learned that we had admitted a fifteen-year-old, Russell Boyd. I thought that he must be socially maladjusted and must have pushy parents. I have changed my mind, however, for two reasons.

First, I have had Russell as a student. Not only did he excel academically, but socially he fit in very well with his classmates. While talking with Russell outside of class, I was impressed not only by his remarkable intellect, but also by his easygoing personality, great sense of humor, and maturity.

Second, I have read Eva Seibert's wonderful little book which explains how she educated her sons Russell and Bobby. Although she did so primarily through homeschooling, finances sometimes dictated that she send her children to public schools in various locations. Thus, Seibert has a unique perspective in comparing various schooling options.

She starts with a common-sense premise: parents love their children more than anyone else and can provide them with the most secure, positive learning environment — one tailored to the individualized needs of each child and designed to help each achieve his fullest potential. Even the best formal school — and Seibert acknowledges several dedicated and competent public school teachers and administrators who helped her children over the years — cannot possibly provide the same benefits as a homeschool.

The real shame is that most professional educators don't even try to meet the needs of bright and energetic students. Seibert recounts many examples of the school system simply maintaining the status quo and focusing on social and athletic development, instead of encouraging and rewarding academic excellence. She also describes how parents like her who complain are treated as ignorant intruders, rather than intelligent and caring partners in their children's educational process.

But this book is not simply another screed against the flawed public school system. Rather, it is a positive story about a single mother who loved her children so much that she was willing to make any sacrifice necessary to ensure that they were educated according to their abilities and that they were provided with age-appropriate social, recreational, and spiritual opportunities.

Seibert fully recognizes the possible dangers of homeschooling. She was very careful in listening to her children and letting them proceed at their own pace. She also acknowledges that homeschooling is not for everyone: many parents cannot do so because of jobs, financial constraints and other factors.

However, for those parents who have the opportunity to educate their children at home, she provides powerful arguments in favor of doing so. My wife Trish and I, who are both professional educators, have discussed the possibility of homeschooling our three children. Even though they attend a very nice Catholic school, we do not feel they are being challenged intellectually. Whenever we mention the homeschool option to family or friends, they invariably look at us as if we've just fallen from Mars. In a well-meaning way, they warn us that homeschooling will turn our children into nerds and social misfits. Seibert's two sons provide concrete evidence that such dire predictions should be taken with a grain of salt.

Eva Seibert tells her fascinating story in an engaging, conversational style. Parents who are thinking about homeschooling their children should read her book. I highly recommend it. It is a real eye-opener.

Professor Robert J. Pushaw

CHAPTER ONE: *A Little Background*

The writing of this book was somewhat unplanned. It was never my intention to undertake several years of homeschooling just so I would have the material to author a book. However, many people have asked me about our story and have encouraged me to write it down. Simplifying our homeschool experiences into a few sub-topics seemed easier than the hit-and-miss conversations I was finding myself engaged in.

I would like to state from the beginning that by writing this book I am in no way professing to be an expert in the field of education — home or otherwise. I am not trying to convince anyone that my way is the preferred way or even that a family should choose homeschooling over other methods of education merely because our experiences intrigue them. I made countless mistakes during our homeschooling tenure, but I also enjoyed countless successes. If by writing this book, I can help others avoid mistakes and enjoy more success, then I'm glad I wrote it.

Talking with people who are interested in homeschooling is one of my favorite things to do. Parents who are investigating the option of homeschooling are usually quite careful with whom they discuss this topic. Fearful of rejection or ridicule, when cautious parents meet someone with whom they can speak comfortably, they become excited and very inquisitive, eager to enjoy all that is good about teaching children (and teaching children is all good).

I am quite happy to spend any time I can answering questions about how we completed certain homeschool tasks. However, I am hesitant about giving advice. What works for one family may prove to be disastrous for another family. Homeschooling in general may not be the answer to everybody's educational dilemmas. In our case it seemed to work. In others cases, different methods of education may be more worthwhile. The only real advice I give freely is don't give up!

If you are considering a homeschool, become aware of factors that would sabotage your efforts. Those factors include becoming distracted by taking up the cause of homeschooling instead of working on the front lines. Distractions will prove detrimental. Remember that your first and most important goal is teaching your children. Do not let yourself become discouraged. Avoid trying to imitate or keep up with the activities in public schools or in other homeschools. Setting unrealistic goals will cause you and your children to become discouraged and uninterested.

Remember that teaching your children should be as stress free and as enjoyable as possible. Making a learning environment peaceful and productive will develop a comfort zone which will last throughout your children's lives. Learning will become a beloved life-long endeavor. But when the learning environment becomes tense, competitive, or labor intensive, the love of learning develops into a thick brick wall of resistance and proves to be a life-long obstacle to success.

If you choose to homeschool — don't give up. I have found while speaking with parents and others who are investigating alternative methods of teaching children, people in general have been programmed to think that their inadequacies in teaching far outweigh the inadequacies of those teaching in our public schools. NOT TRUE!!! At the very least *your* vested interest in *your* children provides you with a deeper insight to the needs of those children. Your history together gives you a foundation for teaching. You have the scope of how much your children already know and this scope gives you a focal point toward which to teach. You love your children. You have hope for their future.

You may decide to place your children in a more traditional classroom setting rather than homeschooling. I did on several occasions. If you do, don't give up! Don't walk away from them. Be very careful not to relinquish total control of your children to those who, although they would probably not intentionally harm them, do not necessarily have their best interests at heart. Your children will always be YOUR children. When they come home from school, make sure you talk with them and find out what took place in the classroom each day. Get specific. Are there areas which need more explanation or clarification or correction (especially in the areas of values or morals or in classroom discipline)? Visit the classroom often. Spend an entire day, maybe even unannounced, if that is what it takes for you to get a clearer picture of the goings on and to be comfortable with the teachings and the teaching styles of your child's public school classroom. Let the teachers and administrators know that you are willing and in fact demanding to have an active role in their daily activities. This isn't always easy and often meets with much resistance. We will spend more time on this subject in a later chapter.

When I was a young girl, my parents took me and my five brothers and sisters out of school for about a year and taught us at home. I am not too sure of the reasons my parents decided to take on the task of homeschooling our family. Their reasons were never made clear to me then or since then. Whatever the reasons were, I know for me it was a very enjoyable year.

I remember writing reports on different countries and studying different animals. I started a vocabulary program to coincide with my spelling words. I learned my multiplication tables. I sat for long periods of time memorizing the states and their capitals. That was the year I learned how to sew. My mother helped me make an apron. I have since developed into a somewhat skilled seamstress.

There were many things I liked about homeschooling. For instance, the home my parents were renting in Phoenix, Arizona, included a swimming pool in the yard. During recess and in the afternoons after our homeschool, we were allowed to go swimming.

The thing I remember most is how much I loved spending time with my mother. I loved reading to her in our living room while she crocheted. I know I loved having the care and attention of my mother. I did not like being in a crowded classroom and being taught by an instructor I knew very little about, except that he knew, or cared, very little about me. I am sure, now, that my instructor in actuality did care about me. But at that time, in my little 10-year-old mind, I was sure that when I was in public school I was very alone. And when I was in homeschool I was just that — very much at home.

I tell you this story because that one year of homeschooling left a favorable impression on me. When the issue arose as an educational alternative in the lives of my children, the idea of homeschooling did not seem strange or socially abnormal.

CHAPTER TWO: *Starting Out*

By 1982, I was a single mother of two boys who were both still in diapers. I had a great deal of time on my hands in the evenings after they finally fell asleep. Each day seemed to be filled with the relentless routine tasks of mothering toddlers. I was active in my church and had many excellent models to pattern my mothering techniques after. I had several friends who were also busy with the role of early childhood development. So this fairly new area — motherhood — was not so much foreign territory as it was undiscovered territory for me. I was not looking for new and exciting ways to accomplish feats never before accomplished. But I was certain that the daily routine of caring for my young children held more than I was experiencing at that time.

While my children were young I didn't think of them as necessarily brilliant. During their toddlers years, I gave little thought about their intellectual growth as it compared to whatever was considered the norm.

Once when my first born, Russell, was about twenty-two months old, I heard him state very articulately and confidently, "Safeway." I was driving through the little Missouri college town we lived in and we had just passed a grocery store. I pulled over to the side of the road and stopped the car. I was astonished because I had never referred to the grocery store by its corporate name "Safeway" but only as "the store." I asked, "What did you just say?" Again, Russell, strapped into his car seat, stretched his little neck so he could peer out the window and said pointing toward the store, "Safeway." I can only assume that he made a name association from television commercials which were running during that time period.

I began noticing what an amazing memory both of my sons were displaying. When my younger son, Bobby, was just eight months old, he was able to bring me things from around the house (toys, pillows, books) after being introduced to these items only once. When Russell was only about eighteen months old, my brother Rick nicknamed him "my little Buddy." When we saw my brother again several months later, he jokingly asked Russell his name. Russell responded "your little Buddy."

I didn't, and still don't consider these instances and many others like them as marks of genius. I only think I was unprepared to recognize them as signs of intellectual potential which I am now convinced *most* children possess.

It wasn't until I came across the book *How to Teach Your Baby to Read* by Dr. Glen Doman, that I began to realize the huge responsibility that would be mine. Children learn and have the ability to learn at a much younger age and a much higher level than I, or society in general, previously gave them credit.

I read Dr. Doman's book several times over. First, I read it to satisfy my intense curiosity. The idea that small children, even babies, had the capabilities to learn and retain what they learn had never before been presented to me.

Next, I read it to analyze the program methods so to be very sure that the techniques taught were in keeping with my religious standards. At the time, plenty of warnings were floating through the nation (and just as many made-for-TV movies) about brainwashing programs and sect indoctrination. I am glad I took the opportunity to make this comparison. I have often been accused by well-meaning friends and church leaders of straying too far from the norm and that the undeveloped areas I was leading my children into would prove to be somehow "dangerous."

I read the book again to learn how to present the program to my sons. The book carefully outlines the procedure to present the program to small children. Great pains have been made to ensure that the presentation is as stress free and enjoyable for both the teacher (the parent) and the students (the babies). The results of Dr. Doman's program were amazing.

By the time I actually started the program, Russell was already speaking in short sentences, but Bobby was still developing his sounds into words. Often, as with most parents of babies, I had a difficult time understanding what Bobby was trying to say to me. But I could tell he understood what I was saying to him.

After working with Dr. Doman's program for about two months, I tried an experiment. I took all of the flashcards of the familiar words we were learning and I spread them, face up, across the living room floor. Without any reviewing or preparation, I called Bobby into the room and asked him to show me the flashcard that said "balloon." He didn't hesitate. I watched his small chubby body dressed only in a diaper, crawl over several flashcards, studying each one while his bottle dangled from his clinched teeth. He stopped on the flashcard labeled balloon, picked it up and started to squeal. I was astonished. As soon as Bobby saw the approval in my reaction he wanted to play again. To be quite certain that the results were no accident, I repeated the experiment several times. By now Bobby's older brother wanted some of the action.

That day both Russell and Bobby completed this exercise, which soon became a game, with 100% accuracy. Both boys enjoyed the feeling of accomplishment as we played our new game. Often, we added interesting and more challenging words to our stack of flashcards. Within a few weeks they graduated from flashcards to easy big print books which contained words my sons were, by then, familiar with. Both boys quickly learned that words form sentences and sentences form thoughts and stories.

Up to this point, I had not invested a lot of effort into any type of educational activities for either one of my boys. I had introduced simple concepts, colors, shapes, new toys, new words, etc., but I had never considered introducing any type of thoughtful learning activities to them. The realization that my children were capable of learning more than I was presenting to them led to some provocative decisions on my part.

I started to do my homework. A lot of it. I read everything I could get my hands on. Each evening as the boys slept, I studied different approaches to teaching, especially teaching young children. I read manuals from college libraries about early childhood development. I checked out books from my local library on subjects dealing with current trends in education. *Parents* magazine had many interesting articles about trends in preschools and day care centers. I learned how information can be presented to children so the learning process won't be slowed or confused.

About this time in my research, a friend passed along an audio cassette tape which would prove to be a turning point in the educational direction I had assumed with my two sons. The tape was titled *Private Schools: A Seedbed For Greatness,* by Reed Benson, Ph.D. While I listened to the tape I was frozen with interest. The material presented by Dr. Benson outlined concerns and apprehensions about the educational situation in America. I had become uneasy with the idea of turning my children over to the standard public schools especially after my research had led me to conclude that the average curriculum was somewhat short-changing the childhood population.

On the tape, Dr. Benson described his experience homeschooling his six children. His counsel was clear and complete. I have yet to find a more complete list of reasons to homeschool than is outlined on that tape. As I listened, I was filled with a new spirit of motivation. Could I homeschool my two sons?

I continued to research different methods of teaching, not necessarily just homeschooling. I realized that the learning atmosphere and the method of presenting new material is of utmost importance. When people learn, children included, they need to learn in an environment that is non-threatening. This concept was a revelation to me.

I remember times in my life when the atmosphere I was expected to learn under was chaotic, competitive and condescending. These were times when I didn't perform to my potential. My retention was shortened and most information presented seemed to confuse me.

I distinctly remember sitting in a classroom in a hot Arizona elementary school during second grade. My teacher was sarcastic and degrading. I avoided asking questions out of fear of being ridiculed. I looked around the classroom often trying to keep up with my classmates. I was very unsure of myself. Most of the time I needed to be reassured that I was on the correct page or even in the same book as other class members. At times when I glanced around to check to see if I was doing the correct worksheet, I was accused of copying. Often I was reprimanded. The fear of the consequences of performing poorly only heightened my insecurities and diminished any efforts I made to keep up with the rest of my class, much less excel.

My anxiety about my teachers and their teaching methods were compounded by my insecurity around my peers. The competitive environment created at school acted as a deterrent for productive learning. I felt inferior to others in areas of athletics and fashion.

I don't remember an excitement to learn or feelings of accomplishment. I am sure, now, the feelings I had were exaggerated with immaturity. But at the time I felt them, they were very real and very much in proportion.

My research revealed the idea that most people are able to receive and retain new information if that information is presented in a calm, positive method. Most people, especially children, are more eager to learn when the learning environment is loving, accepting, encouraging and free from competition, sarcasm, condescension and punishment. That is not to say we should not at times honor outstanding accomplishments or constructively point out areas for improvement. But the way in which this is done is critical to the progression of the learning process.

Although the concept of homeschooling is no longer considered new or radical, few people I have talked with have a middle-of-the-road opinion of homeschooling. Most people are either very much in favor of homeschooling or they are very much against it. Either way, they usually have a long list of reasons to support their viewpoint.

I have a long list of my own. I developed this list throughout the past fifteen years while teaching my children at home and observing the activities of others teaching my children during those times when I resorted to enrolling them in public schools.

My reasons for considering homeschooling included the level of direct attention I afforded my children during the schooling hours of the day. The care I could give them with respect to their self-esteems proved overwhelmingly superior to any attempt made by someone outside our family. I knew I could correct and instruct them without making them feel ridiculed or condemned. I knew I could be much more affectionate and rewarding than could a stranger and appropriately so. I wanted to claim the privilege of teaching my own children and growing with them instead of away from them. I wasn't sure that the value system that the boys were being taught was in keeping with the same standards we upheld as a family. I did not want to risk diluting our values with those that were merely "acceptable" to society.

After our success with reading, I started introducing a few simple educational activities to my two sons. I began noticing their development and appetite for more and more information. I learned to provide my children with educational activities in a game-like manner. When they participated, they never distinguished the educational activities from playing. Many times I introduced something new and then was plagued with pleas to repeat the activity as if to play the game over and over. They would show the same excitement about a new book at reading time as they would for playground time outside, or for music time just before naps.

Both boys learned to print the alphabet while tracing the letters on index cards during church services. Luckily for me this also kept them occupied and quiet. They looked forward every Sunday to learning the shapes and sounds of a new set of letters. Teaching them about their community became weekly field trips to area work places. Math was fun. Counting the cherries in a game of *Hi-Ho Cherry-O* was as enjoyable as dot to dot numbering pictures. Even word problems became game-like. The boys couldn't get enough.

I knew my discoveries were no different from those of most parents. I often asked other parents to share what their children were doing and on what levels they were doing them. I did this not so much to compare or boast about my children's accomplishments as I did to see if my sons were at least on or about on the same level of performance. I think that much of a young parent's life is defined by the children who take up so much of their time. It becomes very natural to talk about the goings on in their children's lives and to bounce ideas off of other parents. However, the more information I introduced to my children and the more I emotionally reinforced what they learned, the more I could tell that they moved educationally faster than their peers.

In time I started to hold back on some of the conversations with other parents. I knew that what I would say bordered on bragging. Instead, I tried to listen and to take mental notes of my observations.

Physically, the boys were on the same level as their friends of the same age. Socially, I could not tell that their development was any more skilled. Academically, however, I could tell that after providing them with only a few months of thoughtfully prepared educational activities, both Russell and Bobby were considerably more advanced than their peers.

I think it is a tricky thing to talk about the observations you make concerning your children because not many parents receive comparative information without inferring competition. The "I can top that..." tendency quickly becomes offensive.

The trick is to contain your excitement about the activities and accomplishments of your children while discussing them with others. But I was excited. Very excited. I had never wondered nor ever had reason to wonder about the intelligence of babies until I had mine. I wanted to talk with everyone about what I was discovering about my children.

Several years later, when my sons were well out of their infant years, an article was printed in the July 1993 issue of *Life* magazine. The title of the article was "The Amazing Minds of Infants." The headline on the front cover of that issue immediately caught my attention. It read: "Babies Are Smarter Than You Think." The subtitle read: "They can Add before they can Count. They can Understand a hundred words before they can Speak. And, at three months their powers of Memory are far greater than we ever imagined." Finally, I held in my hands confirmation of what I had discovered but was up to that point reluctant to share with anyone. Infants carry an insatiable appetite for knowledge, and the way we feed them intellectually can and will determine their academic and educational potential while they grow and at maturity. I recommend this article to anyone who is curious about their baby's capacity to learn.

I should point out that while I encourage others to investigate their children's intellectual potential and provide meaningful educational challenges for them, I am not advocating undue pressures to excel. I think too often adults want so much for their children that they try to push them to meet the standards they themselves wish they could have met. I have seen this often in sports, music and also in education. But I know that pressure to succeed is a very relative thing. What seems to be pressure to some parents is mere encouragement to others.

Many times I was discouraged by the lack of excitement others shared in my family's education. I have often been warned by public educators not to let my children advance so quickly because the long-term results will prove to be socially and/or emotionally harmful. I was clued in to the disadvantages of letting my children think that they could achieve things easier and faster than their age group usually averaged. "I'm just trying to help," or "I just don't want them to grow up to be nerds" were comments I constantly endured.

Many times these comments were from parents whose children were rewarded for being at the top of their public school classes academically. Socially, their children were active to the point of exhaustion. And physically, they participated competitively in every in-season sport, often times serving as presidents of their organizations and/ or captains of their teams.

Now I'm not suggesting that any of these achievements are bad things to accomplish. I am merely pointing out that pressure is a very relative thing.

Allowing children to learn at their own pace and providing them with information as quickly as they are ready to receive and retain it, in an environment that is loving and inclusive as opposed to competitive and exclusive, sometimes results in accelerated levels of accomplishments. Pressure? Maybe. But pressure as compared to what?

In our home during an average day of homeschool, we enjoyed the luxury of avoiding the daily "*hurry up and get to school on time*" run-around. The boys could be given assignments and instructions to complete certain tasks before the end of the day. I tried to tailor their assignments to their personal interests and to provide them with as much individual instruction as was needed to complete these tasks. Often times as we reviewed an assignment, long conversation relating personal experiences would result. The assignments often were bonding, and our family was strengthened.

When something seemed interesting we investigated it even if the public schools didn't usually offer that subject until several years later. When the assignments were completed, we reviewed them together and corrected what needed to be corrected. There was no grading system. What was wrong was corrected and what was right was acknowledged. There were no class levels.

Sometimes our homeschool days would begin by discussing what we wanted to learn that day. We let the boys' interests guide us instead of completing predetermined worksheets and assignments that would prepare them only for certain public standard achievement tests.

To include physical fitness into our homeschool the boys enrolled in town little league sports. They also played outside with the neighborhood children. To include music into our homeschool, the boys enrolled in music lessons. They also participated in singing at church each Sunday, performing in children's choir at least once a year, sometimes more often.

When I think of pressure my mind does not immediately turn to time spent teaching and learning with my children, nor am I reminded of my homeschool days as a child. I do, however, remember exhausting semesters in public school being filled with varying degrees of pressure.

Providing young children with a wide range of experiences and then letting them progress and/or excel at their own pace may seem to those outside of the experience to be pressure. My hope is that by allowing my children room for self-discovery, I *pressured* them right into a life of contentment, healthy self-esteems, and a love of learning.

CHAPTER THREE: *Introduction of School*

During the first few years of my children's lives I took classes part time at local community colleges to improve my employment opportunities. By the time Bobby and Russell were four and five, I decided to enroll in college full time. To do this I also had to place my sons into a daycare center while I attended classes.

The experience at the day care center was a real eye-opener for me. To that point, I had dedicated about three years to conscientious learning activities for the boys. When they started to attend the daycare center, their advanced academic level was quickly made obvious to the daycare providers. Almost immediately the directors of the center called me in to discuss their observations.

Both boys were described as being accelerated well beyond their peer group. The teachers described how both boys were adapting well and getting along with the other children. They acted happy and seemed to liked coming to "day school" each day. Then the teachers described something I hadn't expected.

They told me that on occasion, when they would need to leave the reading circle to tend to an interruption, they could ask either one of my sons to pick up reading aloud where they left off. Both boys were reading stories to a group of three- and four-year-olds. These stories were ones that neither Russell nor Bobby had ever read before. Russell was often found teaching some of the other children their colors or shapes, and Bobby would read individually to other children when they would bring him a book that interested them.

The teachers informed me of the way they each could play diplomatically with their friends and try to maintain peace during playground squabbles. I was happy to hear about their academic progress and even happier to learn how well they were adjusting socially.

By late August, the year Russell was five, I decided it would be more convenient to put him in a public school kindergarten class rather than homeschooling him. I was still single and I was trying to scratch out a living for the three of us. I felt it would be easier on the budget, and on the baby-sitter, if I put him in school for half a day.

I knew Russell was ready for more challenging material than was being offered in kindergarten so prior to this decision I investigated a private school. I was hoping that a private school which accepted children who tested in the intellectually gifted ranges would be able to offer Russell the higher educational challenges while paying attention to his physical and social levels. Although both boys were tested and accepted at the private school, scholarships were limited and my budget couldn't afford the $3000 tuition.

My next alternative was the local public school. So I put Russell in school and pondered at length whether I was doing the right thing for him and our family. It didn't take long for me to be called into the counselor's office of his elementary school to discuss his progress. Russell was creating quite a stir. Nearly all of the assignments given to the classroom seemed to be well below Russell's potential. As it turned out, he would quickly finish his work then move over to the next child's desk and finish his or her assignments too.

Nobody thought Russell was doing this to be rude. He explained that he was trying to help them get done so they, the class, could go on to the next item of business.

I didn't want to tell Russell to slow down or not to excel. The kindergarten teacher didn't want to give too much more outside of her lesson plan. So together, the counselor, Russell and I decided to move Russell on to first grade.

At this particular school there was one first/second grade combination class. The instructor geared the lessons toward children who learned quickly. The teacher of this class was willing to individually structure the lessons to suit each child's needs. This class seemed to fit Russell's needs because the lessons were presented at higher learning levels.

I was still bothered by some of the methods used in teaching. I am not at all saying that the teacher herself was inadequate. I was very impressed with her and her ability to give children anything she could possibly give. But there was still the structured and regime-like atmosphere that never surfaced at home.

Russell was and still is a very slow eater. Lunch was only twenty minutes and he did better with thirty-five or forty. Russell liked learning in the mornings and playing outside in the afternoons. These changes in his daily routine were showing up in his behavior at home. He was tired most of the time. His usually cooperative disposition was replaced with a short temper and tears. Although advancing a grade suited him academically, he still needed his nap in the early afternoons. His attention span shortened during the time he usually napped, and naps are omitted in public schools by the first grade.

Because of these hesitations, and because of other concerns, that year Russell only spent one semester in school. I brought him back home and settled for part-time employment. To finish out the year, we returned to the daily routine we had established before we tried public school. We were happier, although a little less wealthy.

The cautious objections of friends and relatives warned me that by homeschooling the boys I was stripping them of social contact. Social contact. At age five? I was very active in my church, and the boys participated in the Children's Primary Program. We had plenty of friends, and they had fun doing things with other children their ages. I observed both boys getting along with their peers quite normally so the concerns of social deprivation didn't strike me as a problem. Neither of them were — and still aren't — angels. However, the same could be said about the other little boys and girls who attended public schools. Still, the older the boys grew, the more I was growing weary of resisting well intended "advisors" who thought I should put them in a public school setting.

The next year I was offered employment in a small town in southern California. I packed up the boys and moved to accept a sales potion with a swimming pool company. Because I worked mostly in the evenings when my customers were home from work, I was allowed to stay home with the boys during the day. That spring and summer were enjoyable ones. We went on several day trips to lakes and parks. We visited historic sites and museums. We went to San Diego several times to see the attractions and each time ended the day at the beach. We visited upstate California driving through the wine country and exploring San Francisco. We still remember fondly standing on the Golden Gate Bridge.

We never stopped our daily homeschool lessons though. I tried to implement the ideas I had learned in my research of early education.

I spent quite a bit of time cutting bulletin board decorations out of construction paper to appeal to the boys' visual stimulation. I shopped at the teachers' supply stores to find the newest and the most fun ways to introduce new themes and concepts for our lessons. The boys always had assignments. Reading was a daily event and we visited the library three times a week.

As the end of that summer approached, I was again swayed by friends to reconsider public schooling over homeschooling. Each time the subject of the boy's education arose, concerns for their social well being was the main topic. These concerns, most of the time unsolicited, planted seeds of doubt as to my own abilities to offer my children the level of scholastic and social experiences that the schools could offer them.

I visited the local elementary school to get a perception of the atmosphere. Both the teachers Russell and Bobby would be assigned to were pleasant and seemed to be more than competent. The classrooms were brightly decorated, and each desk was adorned ready to welcome the students to the first day of school. The atmosphere seemed exciting. The boys were accepting of the idea of giving public school a try and even excited about new clothes, new friends and new lunch boxes. My apprehensions about public schools subsided somewhat, and my feelings of doing the boys a disservice by keeping them at home heightened. So, compromising my intuition, I enrolled Russell age six and a half into a combination second/third grade class. Bobby at age five would be in kindergarten.

As soon as the school year began, Bobby and I were both ready to quit. I was very unhappy about the way the instructors were scheduled to teach the class. The school was trying out a pilot program of dual teaching. The hours for the half-day class were split during the week between two instructors. I learned that this was some type of flex-time program. But the lessons didn't seem to be very consistent.

Also, I was immediately offended about the way the instructors received the children at the door of the classroom, halting the parents from entering. Insisting that the less time spent on the parent-child separation point the better it was for the children. O.K., maybe. But Bobby had never been in such a strictly structured school environment prior to that time, and the whole scene seemed confusing to him and upsetting to me. Except for parents day, the teachers discouraged visits from the parents, claiming the distraction of the visits was too hard on the structure of the day.

The material being introduced to the kindergarten class was material Bobby had mastered in our home school long before that time. He came home each night expressing extreme boredom, stating that the only thing he liked about school was playground time. I scheduled a time to meet with the instructors of the class. We discussed the possibility of advancing Bobby into first grade so he would be introduced to more challenging material.

I knew that this put him into the same awkward circumstance as was Russell's first grade advancement, but it seemed the only alternative to letting Bobby stagnate in boredom for a full year. The teachers agreed to the advancement only after I agreed to let Bobby be tested for aptitude. I do not think I would have allowed him to be tested if I had known at the time that the testing would last approximately ten days. The tests were long and tiresome. Bobby scored well above kindergarten level in every area of testing and scored as high as fourth and fifth grade level in some areas such as sequencing, reading, and math.

Bobby was advanced, much to the reluctance of the kindergarten instructors. Fortunately, Bobby's first grade teacher turned out to be a friend from church. Her understanding of the whole situation soothed my fears and, except for the physical drain and some moral eye-openers, for Bobby the first semester went well.

Russell was having a good time at school. However, there also were some concerns with his situation. Because he had been advanced to a combination second/third grade class when he chronologically would have been ready for first grade, his classmates were older, stronger, and physically more ready for the strains of the activities assigned to them. Although Russell progressed through the semester with high marks academically, he was showing signs of stress from the physical demands of his class.

Some other things happened that year at school. Outbreaks of lice were common, and I didn't feel at all good about the chemical solutions prescribed for preventing my children from being affected by the outbreaks. News reports gave information about neurological disorders that resulted from the use of such chemicals.

Discipline is always a problem when you assemble that many youngsters into a single room with one custodial leader. Sometimes the tough decisions made during a discipline call are not popular ones. At times, the consequence for an offense was a blanket classroom punishment, punishing the innocent in order to include the guilty in the punishment.

That year in upstate California some deranged person opened fire onto a children's school yard playground, killing many of them. So when a child brought a pocket knife to school, the topic of weapons and self defense was introduced to the young class and so were many rumored stories and visual interpretations that accompany weapon offenses. There was also the time when I dropped the boys off at school and was met by a police officer stating that there had been a child abduction attempted the previous day and security was being stepped up.

Academically both boys were achieving above average scores on all their work. According to their teachers, neither of them had problems relating to their classmates socially, and they both seemed to abide by all the school rules. By semester's end though, exhaustion set in and neither of the boys hesitated when I offered the option of homeschool. So once again I withdrew my sons from the school system and brought them home. There were things we missed about public school, more free time for me and some friends for the boys. But the advantages homeschool offered outweighed the disadvantages enough to stay right where we felt most comfortable. Peace again returned to our home, and our learning environment felt secure.

I was unsure of the decision to withdraw my children from school until a friend of mine passed along a book about a research project conducted on measuring the effects early school enrollment has on children and, in the long run, society. I remembered first hearing about the book on the tape by Dr. Reed Benson. *School Can Wait*, by Raymond and Dorothy More, offered more than a little insight on the subject of early childhood education. The book identifies many negative traits and consequences which surface when a child is taken from a comfortable familiar home environment and then introduced to a structured school environment before that child is physically, socially or emotionally ready. I immediately recognized these traits as ones which surfaced when my sons were in school.

I agree for the most part with the conclusion of the study on which the book was based. However, there were statements in the book that alluded to warnings of offering (somehow pressuring) educational information prematurely. It had been my experience with the boys that they were their best monitors about that issue.

When the boys were introduced to a subject that they were not intellectually ready for, their confusion pointed us back down to a lower subject level We knew when a subject was too difficult or not challenging enough, and we knew how to gauge our own expectations. I still felt that there was nothing mentally or psychologically detrimental about introducing information to children as soon as they displayed an appetite for it and seemed to receive and retain it.

The boys were growing intellectually at a rate that was well beyond the average expectations. I had to decide which would be more of a moral disservice, allowing them to creep along at a slower pace to satisfy the cautious national educational norm or allowing them access to an accelerated education and risking their ending up academically well past their chronological peers.

Another decision which needed to be made quickly was one of curriculum. Was I going to use the same type of course curriculum outlined in the public schools or use one of the homeschool, often Christian-based, curriculums available?

I didn't find the outline of the public school courses particularly attractive, because by then my sons were well past their grade levels of learning in many of the subjects such as math, science and reading. Yet they had not shown interest in some of the other subjects such as history and phonics. As a matter of fact, I couldn't understand why they even needed phonics since they were already reading at fourth and fifth grade levels.

I wasn't sold on the homeschool curriculum offerings either for many of the same reasons. The all-or-nothing subject offerings left little room for personal interests or accelerated rates. Another thing I found with the Christian curriculums is that some other individual's interpretations of religious standards were imposed. I consider myself an active Christian. But what if I were a practicing Jew or Muslim? Some of the editorial remarks in the textbooks were very charismatic. We never really shouted "hallelujah" when we finished a math program or praised God when we finished a chapter in spelling. I'm not saying that there is anything wrong with rejoicing after completing an assignment, but these curriculums just didn't fit our style of learning.

The answer to our curriculum dilemmas came in the form of a 16-page booklet published by World Book, Inc. When I was considering purchasing a set of encyclopedias for my family, the sales representative used a booklet during his presentation. The booklet, entitled *Typical Course of Study,* outlines an overview of courses commonly used in schools for grades K through 12. The outline includes subjects and subject levels normally mastered by the end of each designated school year. The outline was compiled from an analysis of educational programs in representative school systems in the United States. I used the booklet to guide me somewhat in presenting lessons in our homeschool. I wanted to be sure that the boys were learning at least on the academic levels as their chronological peers in the public schools.

Besides curriculums, there was another hesitation I had about homeschooling. I was unsure as to how to measure the success of their education. I had considered letting the boys take the standard achievement test in the public schools. These tests were labor intensive for the boys and were expensive for me. I decided that their scores on standardized tests shouldn't and didn't matter to us as homeschoolers because there is no way a testing mechanism can measure results of learning experiences not accounted for. We had been learning things in our home that were not even being introduced to public schools. Also, how can one measure the success of emotional stability? I would, for the time being, not concern myself with the scores of tests, but rather concentrate my concerns on the educational well being and the emotional happiness of my sons.

After living in southern California for two years, we longed for home. Experiencing the things we did during our time in the western part of the states left us with countless favorable memories. However the high cost of living, the earthquakes, the pollution and the crime made me hesitant of staying. I decided to make my way back to the Kansas City area where I grew up. Even though my budget and the weather proved to be obstacles of sorts, the two-week trip back to the Midwest was filled with sight-seeing and visiting friends. During the trip, I grew closer to my two sons, and we were able to visit many exciting places (the Planetarium in Salt Lake City, the Grand Canyon in southern Utah and northern Arizona., Heard Indian Museum in Phoenix, the Hard Rock Cafe in Dallas, etc.).

I realized during the trip home that other children may never be afforded the opportunities that result from the flexibility of homeschool. My children were growing intellectually, culturally and socially. The realizations I made during this trip gave me renewed motivation to continue my efforts in homeschooling and gave me a new degree of strength to resist "encouragement" toward public schools.

CHAPTER FOUR: *Back and Forth*

After returning to Kansas City, Missouri, I was hard pressed to find employment which offered me the same flexibility as did my sales job with the swimming pool company. Although relying on straight commissions is not easy, in sales I was able to set my own appointments and adapt my schedule to my needs. This flexibility allowed me time to teach the boys.

Now in Kansas City, I couldn't find the type of job which would afford me the same luxuries in my schedule and also provide a constant income for my family. Fortunately for me and the boys, we were able to live with a very supportive and patient mother.

For the better part of two years, I accepted part-time jobs, most times at odd shifts, in order to keep to my commitment of homeschooling. I was by this time more committed than ever. If there were a few items for concern in the California school system, there was an avalanche of concerns in the Kansas City School system. The polarization of opportunities was appallingly obvious. Some schools we visited within the system were displaying the best of the best in public school facilities. Yet others were lacking in the basic safety and physical facilities fundamental to operating a successful school.

One modest yet amazingly productive school I would like to mention is the Crestview Elementary School in North Kansas City. Cautiously and reluctantly, I enrolled the boys there when I decided to work longer hours. I needed to pay some mounting bills.

While the boys attended there, I saw everything that was good about public education. The administrators knew each child by name as well as most of the names and occupations of the children's parents. I'm sure a sincere effort was made to catch a glimpse of the home life of each child in attendance. By now Bobby was in second grade. His teacher Mrs. Annie Hughes, as loving and patient as she was competent, was from a large family, and was working on her Ph.D. Russell, a third grader, had Mrs. Barbara Nelson who immediately made Russell feel at ease. She maintained a welcome level of serenity in her classroom. In both classrooms the children seemed happy, and I could tell the subjects were being taught with enthusiasm and with positive reinforcement. I was at this time working part-time as a cake decorator. I tried to schedule my hours so I could go to the school with the boys. I offered to help the teachers and assist in any way I could. Sometimes I would grade papers. Sometimes I would listen to a reading group. But always I was welcomed into the classroom.

These visits accomplished three things. First, I was put at ease about where my children were during the day and what they were filling their time with. Second, the visits allowed my children the chance to see that I was still very close to them. I knew what was happening with them daily, and I felt they still needed emotional support from the home front. Third, the visits allowed me to support the teachers by showing them that I was willing to act in partnership in the education of my children. The teachers were able to communicate with me on almost a daily basis. I valued their mantel as teachers, and I believed they valued mine as parent.

Unfortunately for us, we were only able to stay at that superb elementary school for one semester. My finances were looking up, and I rented a little house only six blocks away from where we were staying. Although the distance was a short one, it was a far enough move to land us into the territory of a different elementary school. The last week at Crestview was a sad one. The boys had made some fun friendships, and they were truly going to miss everything about their little school. The teachers and the principal wished they could make an exception to the boundaries, but rules are rules and we said our goodbyes.

I am very fortunate to have had that one semester experience with my boys there at that little known, worn-down but not worn-out elementary school. Both boys seemed very happy with their classroom activities and their teachers. Although we knew that some of the lessons would cover things they already knew, the teachers made the rest of the classroom activites so interesting that my sons completely enjoyed their time there.

I know that however few and far between, there are some elementary schools that seem to be able to meet every expectation, every parent's standard in social and educational growth. Those are the types of schools that deserve the high respect that I rarely hold for public schools. Most of the schools we had visited had more wrong with them than right. I didn't have the time nor the energy to try to correct all the things I saw that were wrong. But at that time, in my mind and in my heart, Crestview Elementary school had more right, and the things wrong were so insignificant I can't think of any. My thanks.

The experience at the new school turned out to be not so noteworthy. The atmosphere was cold, militant, punitive, restrictive, and the excitement and the fun of learning seemed to be replaced with routine busy work. The children didn't seem to be as free-spirited. The teachers were inflexible about their structure, and the whole picture seemed very regime-like, resembling a rank and file military campus. Warning signs immediately waved, and I removed the boys from that school after a record two-day attendance.

I was frustrated over the differences between the two recent school experiences. How could the two schools be so opposite? We were in the same school district, same mission statement, same school board and superintendent. I think some of the new and progressive schools with their money and impressive attendance could probably take a few lessons from the faculty and staff and those who are on the front lines in the schools which, although lacking in manpower and money, lack nothing in the areas of genuine concern for children.

Once again I began the enjoyable yet taxing job of teaching my sons at home. They were getting older by then. The constant teaching was lessening, and more independent study was being assigned. I should point out that I was never sorry to take on the task of teaching my children. But, I was also very much aware of how much time and energy was invested in the undertaking. Although the students may be finished with their assignments, the teacher goes on to prepare for upcoming lessons (all the while maintaining the home and the laundry and nutritious meals, and the budget). I often thought how it would be so much more convenient and financially prosperous if I enrolled the boys into school full time so I could train for and pursue a career. Many of my friends and family members also thought the career avenue was in our best interest and never hesitated to express their opinions. But it didn't take much to bring me back to reality.

The emotional happiness and stability of one's family is worth the sacrifice of any career. There was rarely a time when I wasn't tired, but at least I wasn't sick with stress and worry over my children's well-being. We were nearly always broke, but because everything was right with our home and the boys were happy and healthy, we were never poor.

Even at this point in the boy's education I could be easily swayed into public schooling. Although my intuition urged me otherwise, I sometimes let the more "knowledgeable" convince me of the advantages of public schooling and "enlighten" me about the disadvantages of homeschooling. It wasn't until several years later as I witnessed the amazing positive results homeschooling had on my sons that I developed the courage to stand by my beliefs.

For me and my family, homeschooling was the best alternative because I was the authority on what was best for *my* children.

After some time, I accepted a job with an answering service in Kansas City, Kansas. The wage was significantly higher than what I had been earning, and the company was located in a very attractive area of the city. I found a nice affordable apartment and a roommate who agreed to stay with my children while I worked the night shift in exchange for her portion of the rent. Another attractive factor about this move was that my new apartment was located in an area of Kansas which had a nationally ranked school system. I was still teeter-tottering about homeschooling and didn't become headstrong until much later.

The state of Kansas at this time was not as accommodating to homeschoolers as was Missouri, so the decision to place the boys in school was an easier one. They would begin at the start of the spring semester. When I went to enroll the boys, I thought I could make things easier on all concerned parties by enrolling them into the grade levels that they would normally, chronologically, be placed. However, the school counselors had some major hesitations about admitting them so easily into those grade levels after being home taught without sufficient testing. They needed scholastic evidence that the boys were up to the same educational levels as were their peers. I was certain that the material being introduced in these classes would be at levels which the boys could adapt to easily. But the *authorities* at the school insisted on intensive testing before they could determine at what grade levels to admit my sons.

Initially, I was offended that the school administrators would somehow not believe me when I tried to convince them that both boys were well prepared for the material which was being introduced in their respective grade levels. After all, I was just the parent. What could I possibly know about the educational experiences of my children? However, the school officials eased my resistance when they explained that recently they had admitted some homeschooled children who were well below the levels of materials that were being presented in the classrooms. After some convincing I allowed my sons to be tested.

The test results were very enlightening to me and to the school authorities. Both boys scored well above the national average for all of the five subjects tested. In addition to the subject testing, the school also tested Russell and Bobby for an Intelligence Quotient (IQ). Although scores didn't and still don't mean a whole lot to me, their results were amazing. Both children tested extremely high. When the boys were finally admitted to the elementary school, they were accepted into the gifted programs.

During the time that the boys attended the schools in Kansas they participated in some of the best educational programs that public schools have to offer. The screening of the faculty and staff was superb, and the teachers came well qualified. The economic situation for the area was well above the national average, and the financial advantages were immediately obvious. The administrators, as well as the facilities, were profiled by Dan Rather on CBS's *48-Hours* as being ranked the "best in the nation." The school was carpeted throughout, the gym equipment was new and top of the line, and the library was as complete as I had ever seen. I was sure that there was not another public school that my sons could attend that could offer more in its facilities and educational programs than this one.

But there were some drawbacks to attending school in such an economically privileged area. Both Russell and Bobby quickly became painfully aware of their inability to actively participate with their peers in activities not associated with school but promoted through the school. Soccer, for instance, is a very popular sport for both boys and girls in this part of the city. Neither one of my sons could participate in the same soccer leagues as their classmates because of my financial limitations. My financial limitations also made it impossible for my sons to wear the same name-brand clothing that their friends were wearing. Before this point I was sure that children of their ages didn't pay attention to clothing labels, but I was immediately enlightened.

The false sense of value placed on fashion and on athletics were not my only concerns while my children attended this school. I was apprehensive about the trend I witnessed with regard to providing young children with such ridiculously unproportioned rewards for academic achievements. Money, clothes, parties and computer games were just some of the rewards given by well intending parents for their children's good report cards. But I think the mother who offered a trip to space camp to her son for getting a good grade in science wins the award "for most outrageous in a supporting role."

I also had mixed opinions about the academic competitions sponsored by the schools. I was pleased that my children were invited to participate in math and spelling relays. They usually made it into the finals. I was very happy when Russell was invited to compete in the nationally acclaimed Odyssey of the Mind competitions. Although the results were impressive (Russell's Odyssey of the Mind group won first in the state of Kansas for the spontaneous problem-solving category), the level of stress which accompanied the competitions didn't seem to balance the rewards for having participated. It was at events such as these competitions that I established my philosophy that pressure to achieve was a relative issue. I witnessed demanding parents *encouraging* their children to succeed. I watched as students cried when they realized the mistakes they made had eliminated them from such prestigious competitions. I decided soon after witnessing these events that my children, however beneficial they may be to the school's overall rating, would participate in school competitions only at their own request and only until it stopped being fun.

CHAPTER FIVE: *Small Town Sentiments*

Up to this point in time, I had tried to work at jobs which allowed me to spend as much time with my two sons as possible. I had accepted jobs such as cleaning houses, mowing lawns, ironing, babysitting, adult day care, cake decorating and typing. It seemed important to me that both boys continue to have the love and attention from at least one of their parents. Visits from their father were few and far between.

The fact that the boys saw their father only about five times during their first fourteen years makes me glad that I chose sporadic jobs and settled for what seemed to be chronic underemployment. Although the responsibility of their temporal well-being was important, I never apologized for refusing to neglect the emotional and intellectual needs of my sons.

After some time, the answering service company began to go through several managerial changes, and my part-time hours didn't fit their schedule. So after the year lease was up on my apartment, I decided not to renew for another year. I moved to a small town in Missouri with a population of about 1,000 people.

This town had a lot of heritage. Most of the residents were related to each other or had family who had lived there for decades. We received a very warm welcome from some in the little community about 45 miles east of Kansas City. There were some, however, who never could warm up to us and made living in that small town very uncomfortable. I was happy to escape the busy rush of the city and glad that the values on clothing and material wealth were not as apparent there as they seemed to be in the city. The community was mainly an agricultural one, and the network of town and school administration resembled a good ol' boy system. Still, I was happy to try a slower, easier atmosphere.

The day I visited the schools in our new town I was left with some major concerns. At the entrance of each door in the school there hung a posted warning that asbestos had been found during a recent building inspection. The sign instructed any party wanting more information to contact the superintendent. I did. His answers to my questions were extremely evasive. I asked him to explain exactly when and where had the asbestos been found, what measures were being taken to cure the problems, and what were the health factors that I should be aware of concerning asbestos. Trying to be as tactful as possible, I asked these questions several times over and each time received very wordy, evasive, run-around type of answers.

I was immediately discouraged. I remember wondering, "Why won't this man, who supposedly is the chief administrator of the school functions and facilities, give me any clear and concise answers? Shouldn't the superintendent, of all people, be straightforward with parents, and shouldn't he have the utmost concern for the well -being of the students who attend that school?" It was evident to me that day that I was not going to receive any straightforward answers about this problem, so I decided to pursue my questions another time. I wanted to concentrate my attention on the rest of the visit.

My observations from the rest of the visit didn't prove to be any less discouraging. When I first approached the elementary school office, I found the school's secretary taking several students' temperature using the same thermometer without using thermometer shields. She explained to me that the school didn't have a nurse, as she read one student's temperature, dipped the thermometer into a bottle containing the remains of some rubbing alcohol and proceeded to the next ill student. The office was very small, and several teachers were stumbling around each other to get access to the office supplies and copy machine which were kept in the same office.

I explained that I was here to visit the school. The secretary asked if I was from 'the state.' I said I wasn't. She asked me if I was doing an inspection. Again I said I wasn't and told her I was merely visiting the school because I was considering enrolling my children. She introduced herself as the school secretary and gave me an Avon brochure and told me that she was also an Avon representative, so if there was anything I needed she could have it to me by the end of the week. I thought to myself "O.K., but I'd still like to tour the school." I asked if it would be possible to visit with the principal.

The principal was kind and seemed happy at the prospect of two new students attending the school. I was allowed to visit with the teacher my oldest son would be assigned to. She was pleasant and I felt confident about her abilities as a teacher. But by the end of the visiting the school, I still felt hesitant with the decision to enroll Russell and Bobby. I had some major concerns about the things I noticed during the visit. I was in need of support from the schools. I was not so much concerned with my children missing out on educational and intellectual opportunities. I was in need of a place for them to stay while I found more stable employment. By then my decision to work only part-time temporary jobs had left me financially desperate. I knew I could no longer dedicate so much of each day to teaching my children. I had to accept at least a permanent part-time job in a neighboring town. Financially, I had no other options. I started to work and put both sons in public school.

Bobby was now in third grade. Although I knew that academically he was beyond the third grade level in many of the subject areas, I felt it would be easier to let him stay with his chronological peers. It was our misfortune to go to a school small enough to have only one teacher presiding over the entire third grade.

Dealing with the teacher Bobby was assigned to that year was, without a doubt, the worst experience we have had throughout our public school attendance. This particular teacher had been teaching by then for nearly twenty-five years. The whole "children should be seen and not heard" philosophy was strictly enforced. Bobby related experiences in which his teacher belittled, demeaned and ridiculed the third-graders. Bobby came home with reports of students being hit by the instructors or having outrageous punishments for stepping out of line. I approached the administration with concerns on several occasions. As one could imagine, the grapevine in a school of this size is quite extensive. So each time I would inquire about any number of the teacher's behavior, Bobby would immediately feel the punitive repercussions in class.

My work schedule at my new job rotated. On the days when I was scheduled in the evenings, I decided to go to school with Bobby to sit in on his class.

I started with short visits, one or two hours. I didn't see too much evidence to support Bobby's claims of classroom abuse. Bobby, as well as other classmates, would tell me later that when I visited, the teacher was on good behavior. Bobby also told me that as soon as I would leave the classroom, the teacher would become vindictive against Bobby, saying things such as "if that's O.K. with *you,* Bobby?" after giving an assignment or withholding a fun classroom activity, stating sarcastically, "I would do this for the class if Bobby hadn't run home to tell his *mommy* on me." When Bobby told me of these abuses, I informed the school officials that I would be exercising my right to observe Bobby's class until I was certain that there was no abuse occurring by Bobby's teacher.

I went to class with Bobby nearly every day for two weeks. Most of the two weeks I sat in the back of the room quietly without taking any exception to the way the teacher conducted herself. There were a few times when the teacher was out of line and condescending to other students, for whom I felt compassion and also felt helpless to do much about. During those two weeks, Bobby was happy and productive and reported that the teacher was nicer to him than she had ever been to anyone in the class.

I was later approached by a few of the parents of the other children. Some were not pleased that I was making the teacher feel as if she were being evaluated. I hadn't intended to do so, although now I don't think it is such a bad idea to hold more of our public school teachers accountable for their own bad behavior. Some parents were suspecting the same abuse as I had suspected. Some were thankful and wished they were available or just had the guts to visit the classroom.

Bobby seemed to want to go to school. He was making friends, going to classmates' birthday parties and having friends spend the night on sleep-overs. I was sometimes torn with the decision to step in or back off and hope the classroom abuse would take care of itself. Whenever I eased up on the classroom visits, Bobby would come home with reports of continuing abuse.

By the end of the school year, I was visiting the classroom on a regular basis and/or confronting the school officials nearly every day. I informed the school administration that I was documenting each and every incident that even slightly resembled classroom abuse. I told them that until I was satisfied that the administration was doing everything possible to educate the faculty in the prevention of classroom abuse, I would basically be in their faces for the rest of the year. I was somewhat sorry to have become such a controversial spectacle (others in the school district would probably choose to call me by a different name), but I have never been sorry to stand up for the right of my child to learn in a non-threatening environment. I have since been thanked by several of the parents of Bobby's classroom and even asked to tutor two of his schoolmates.

Fortunately, that year Russell was assigned to one of the school's best teachers. Mrs. Dickie had obviously kept up with productive teaching trends and was aware of the need to treat her students with the same respect she reserved for herself. Russell was able to make friends easily and participated in the class projects.

The school work was simple for him, and in most of his subjects he scored high marks on his report card. Oddly, he scored a "D" in reading. This confused me. I knew Russell was an avid reader. He explained that the reading was boring to him and that he just didn't feel like he wanted to spend extra time on it. I asked why he didn't just spend the time allotted in class. He explained that during the time the class was in reading, he would leave the classroom to attend ALF — Accelerated Learning Fellowship.

The school my sons were enrolled in had a type of gifted and talented class which they both qualified for, ALF. I was concerned though that while the boys would leave their regular classroom to participate in this so-called accelerated program, they were still held accountable for the class work assigned back at their homeroom during this same time period. Often, the gifted class was conducted during a time frame which eliminated one or both of the boys from enjoying recess. I found the programs designed for this gifted class consisted mostly of busywork. The material covered was more difficult than the work offered in their regular classrooms, but it still seemed like busywork. The fact that they had to forfeit recess and continue to be held accountable for their regular classroom work made the disadvantages of participating in such a class outweigh the advantages. The next semester, Bobby chose not to participate in the accelerated class.

One opportunity did present itself that year as part of the gifted class. The instructor had each of the seventh and eighth grade students participate in the Duke University National Talent Search which required the students to take the American College Testing college entrance exam. Neither Russell nor Bobby were eligible to take the test that year since Bobby was in the third grade and Russell was in the fourth. But an interesting thing happened the following year.

CHAPTER SIX: *The Problems with Pageants*

I decided that the academic material that was to be offered to Russell in the fifth grade was still far below what he could intellectually handle. I approached the school administration to ask that Russell be advanced to the grade level which I thought would challenge him and therefore make his school experience more enjoyable. I examined the textbooks which would be used in the upcoming fifth grade and found the material, for the most part, to be review for him. I did the same thing for the textbooks for the sixth grade and came up with the same results.

I wasn't comfortable with the idea of advancing Russell two grade levels because of the physical differences between the two age groups. But I was certain that the academic material which would be presented in the seventh grade would be more appropriate. So the school principal and I hesitantly allowed Russell to skip from the fourth grade to the seventh grade with the understanding that if either of us (me at home and the principal at school) noticed any detrimental consequences of the advancement we would remove Russell from the seventh grade and find a more comfortable fit.

News spread fast throughout the small town where we lived, and Russell began to receive cutting accusations about his advancement. There were hurtful rumors about the advancement being a result of a relationship between me and the principal. Accusations about Russell trying to show off were among many of the mean-spirited comments we all had to endure.

Nevertheless, with only a few exceptions, advancing to seventh grade was a good experience for him. Although he was at somewhat of a disadvantage in P.E., Russell was performing above average in most of his classes. He earned a spot in National Junior Honor Society, and he received high scores in each subject on his report cards.

He was still involved in the gifted class that year. When the time came for the Duke Talent Search, Russell was eligible to take the A.C.T. exam since he was enrolled in the seventh grade. When the results were mailed to him, Russell and I were both surprised to see that his scores were all above the national average for first-term college freshman. At the time, the scores seemed amazing, but they didn't mean very much to us. Later these scores helped in another academic endeavor.

I should point out that during the time my sons were attending this particular public school, I would on occasion agree to substitute for that school district. It seems funny to me now to have had such strong concerns about this specific public school and still agree to substitute. The town was small, and there were not many people who qualified and who were also available on short notice to substitute. Besides, I needed the money. I enjoyed teaching and when I was teaching, the students seemed to receive me well. I was able to observe many aspects of the public schools parents would not normally be privy to.

First, I noticed a distinct difference in the attitudes of the children who came to school obviously fed and well dressed. They were happy, and they seemed to concentrate more easily than the children who came to school looking like they had slept in their clothes and hadn't brushed their hair or eaten breakfast.

I know that not every impression based on the appearance of the children is correct. However, I have few doubts that the children who are successful in school, both academically and socially, for the most part came from homes whose parents paid attention to things like eating habits, sleeping habits and study habits of their children. School was an obvious physical and emotional strain for some of the children in the classes I was teaching. Many times these physical and emotional strains became obstacles to the learning process for these children.

I also noticed that there were physical and emotional strains that were caused by the school environment itself. Once when Russell was playing on the playground after a rainy morning, he hadn't been paying much attention to where he was playing and stepped in a puddle of water. The playground coach told him to go stand by the wall as punishment for breaking one of the playground rules. Not only was Russell new to this school and not aware of the rules (even the ridiculous ones), he hadn't noticed that the playground coach was even speaking to him. The coach had interpreted Russell's disregard of his orders to stand by the wall as being defiant, so he ran to Russell and pulled him to the wall by the hair on the back of his head. Russell was embarrassed and I went ballistic.

That was the day I learned that some schools in America are still under the archaic philosophy of corporal punishment. In that particular school district the standing rule was that if the parent had not written a letter to the school administration informing them that they did not have permission to physically reprimand their child, the school officials assumed the right to discipline children as they saw fit. I thought this policy contradicted the progressive thinking that if children are hit they learn to solve their problems by hitting. I also thought it amazing that so many parents in this community were willing to allow their children to be punished in ways that were completely subjective to the discretion of their teachers. Yes, I did witness children misbehaving, and I have mixed feeling about the way they may have been dealt with. But I am absolutely certain that hitting children is not the answer to any discipline problems.

I immediately wrote a letter to the school officials removing any right to physically reprimand my children and also went so far to insist that when any verbal discipline was necessary, I was to be called in to witness the discipline. This instruction to the school was accompanied with stern warning to both boys that if they misbehaved in school to the point of needing to be disciplined, they would be in store for serious consequences when they got home (mainly extra chores). I never did have a serious problem with discipline.

Another observation I made during my experience as a substitute was the way many parents handed the entire responsibility of the education and social direction of their children over to the schools. I noticed some children coming to school early in the morning to eat breakfast after already being at a before-school day care provider. The students spent all day in the care of teachers and left school to go to more baby-sitters or stay after school for after-school daycare. Some of the students were from disadvantaged circumstances, but others were from families which would be considered privileged. I noticed that when the strain of such schedules would begin to surface in the behavior or performance of these children, the parents would yank their children to counselors who would frequently prescribe drugs for A.D.D. (Attention Deficit Disorder). Hmm? I do think there was attention deficit. But the fact of the matter was, it may have been the parents who were being deficient in the attention they were paying to their children. It is my opinion that this type of attention deficit was more the case than the certifiable learning disability.

As often as I noticed teachers taking abusive, negligent, unfair advantage of classroom discipline, I also noticed as many parents not showing the slightest interest in the school-related portion of their children's lives.

In all fairness, I should say that in every school the boys attended, there were teachers and administrators who worked diligently to provide wholesome, healthy, productive learning environments for the students. And there were parents who supported their children in their efforts and actively participated in supporting their teachers. But I am convinced that the schools are at a disadvantage with more non-interested parents than interested parents. Teachers battle with parents who would relinquish total custodial responsibility to the schools. Often parents blame schools for their children's failures while hoarding all of the credit for their children's success. Maybe more parents should share the academic and custodial responsibility with the school and maintain the majority of moral and social teachings. Somewhere our children are stuck in the middle.

As Russell began seventh grade, Bobby was ready for the fourth grade. Bobby wanted to go to public school in September. It was a fun time for him. He was placed in the same classroom with the same teacher that Russell had the year previously. Things went well. He was voted as male class representative, did well in his studies, made friends and for the most part had a good experience.

When the time came for the school's annual homecoming activities to begin, Bobby was voted fourth grade candidate for the elementary school Homecoming King. I had not been prepared for this type of popularity contest to begin so quickly. He was only in the fourth grade. I was always somewhat opposed to King and Queen contests. I probably developed this adverse opinion since I was never one to be considered royalty material in the schools I went to. Neither were any of my friends. I had always considered these types of contests snobbish to the maximum degree. King or Queen of what anyway? What exactly does that title entitle one to? Is the King or Queen a better person or kinder to those around them as a result of being voted into that position? Usually not.

When Bobby came home and told me that he had been picked as the class candidate, I could tell that he was extremely excited. I talked with him briefly about the situation but did not tell him of my reservations about such contests.

When he told me the procedure of voting I was even more concerned. Apparently the school had a long tradition of using this popularity contest as a fund raiser. Each grade level was to pick a candidate for King and Queen. A glass jar would then be placed in the principal's office — one for each candidate. A picture of the candidate would be glued to the front of the jar and money was collected in each jar. When a student wanted to vote for the candidate they wanted to win, they simply put more and more money into that jar. The proceeds of this fund raiser went to the local chapter of the Future homemakers of America. O.K. Seems simple enough.

The problem with this type of voting procedure was soon apparent to Bobby. He became preoccupied with how much money was in the jars. He was embarrassed and worried that his jar was not the winning jar. He was consumed with the thought of not letting his classmates down. Many of the other candidates were raising far more money in their jars than was Bobby. He mentioned that the candidate who seemed to always be ahead (and eventually won) was the son of a local business owner. That was the first time I remember being embarrassed in front of my son because of the meager financial situation I was in.

One day soon after the contest began, Bobby got an idea to raise extra money for his jar by going door to door in our neighborhood asking for donations to the Future Homemakers of America. Sounded good to me. After a few doors and rejections the idea didn't seem so appealing to him. He quickly decided that playing football in the empty lot behind our house with the neighborhood kids was easier and more fun than trying to get money to fill his jar. He came in, told me he didn't care if he was king or not and went to play football.

I was happy to see that Bobby was not as consumed with winning the title of King as he seemed to be earlier.

The next day, however, Bobby got called into the office and was verbally reprimanded for trying to cheat. "Don't you know that was cheating?" (Oh, right — like having your financially successful parents stuff your jar was fair?), "Don't you know that what you did was against the law?" (What are you going to do — arrest him for trying to raise money for the Future Homemakers?), "Don't you know that by doing what you did you could cause this contest to be canceled in the future?" (Like, by now after fifteen minutes of verbal abuse, Bobby cares about the future of this contest).

I, of course, was not consulted about the horrible crime Bobby had committed against society, and Bobby was too embarrassed to tell me when he got home that day. After noticing that he was quieter than usual and that he didn't even touch his supper, I finally got him to give me the details of his day. Poor little guy. In his little fourth-grade mind he had been convinced that what he had done was probably worse than anything anyone else had ever done before. He was embarrassed, scared and upset.

I tried my best to comfort him. The next day, I went to the school to let the teacher who had reprimanded him feel some of the wrath of that "over-protective" parent I was often accused of being.

I am convinced, now more that ever before, that contests and pageants such as those held at Homecoming and Prom serve no other purpose than to elevate the egos of the "pretty," and in most cases, the privileged.

Another area I constantly see over developed egos is in the area of sports. The praise goes to the schools who value sports programs for just exactly what they are, extracurricular activities.

At the small town school that Russell and Bobby went to, there seemed to be an unbalanced level of attention given to those who excelled athletically over those who excelled academically. Even students who were somewhat behind in their grades were given accolades because they were strong enough to carry the team to a victory. I know of one case where the attendance, classroom performance and conduct of one athlete high school junior was so seriously lacking that it showed up when he attempted to take the A.C.T. At the end of his Junior year he scored a whopping 14. This young man had several police reports written on him for misbehaving during late night parties. Yet, this is also the same young man who was hailed a semester earlier in an honor assembly for citizenship. This example seemed to be the norm and not the exception.

The unbalanced attention of sports over academics also became apparent in the budget. Activities such as geography contests, math bowls and business competitions were under-funded, while the football and basketball teams were well funded and received money not only from the school board, but also from gifts from the community. I can't be positive, but my guess is that not many of the "jocks" were offered Pro status, and the money and attention issued to the sports programs were as dispensable as their sports careers. I would hope that the money and attention given to the academic programs in schools help students develop the knowledge and the skills needed to begin and continue careers and to prepare young people to contribute to society.

Now, I am not contending that there is no room for sports programs in our public schools. I'm not even saying athletic accomplishments should not be acknowledged and/or rewarded. I am merely under the opinion that schools continually fall short in providing the minimum basic skills needed to function in society due to lack of funding. Yet, often these same schools have enough funding for the sports programs to succeed. More people need to know how to read, write and do math, than need to know how to take down a wide receiver.

Another issue that was difficult to contend with during our stay in this small town was the "all-in-the-family" trend. This town had a lot of heritage. Four and five generations of families were embedded deep in the roots of that heritage. Small town folks often have the problem of keeping to themselves and shying away from newcomers and from those who view issues differently than that of the norm.

CHAPTER SEVEN: *Looking at College*

Bobby decided to home school the rest of his fourth grade year. He had a great second semester. We worked out of workbooks, went to the local library, took field trips, enrolled in piano lessons and worked on a lot of art projects.

One week we studied aviation. That week we bought a kite and flew it in the field down the street. This field was near but not on the school property. While we were out flying the kite, the class that Bobby would have been in came out to the playground for P.E. They all witnessed us playing with the kite and smiled, waved and called his name. Bobby called back and waved. He seemed happy to be with me and still have acceptance from his peers. Things seemed to be better for Bobby and his friends when people realized that Bobby was homeschooling as a matter of personal choice and not as an indication that he was somewhat better or different than his peers. Homeschooling was just an option that we tapped into.

Some of our neighbors, however, had a hard time with the concept of home schooling. One day during this same semester of Bobby's fourth grade year, we received a knock at our front door. A state social service worker had come to see if there was any substantial evidence to support a neighbor's anonymous charge of child neglect. The visit was, of course, a surprise. I was happy that the visit took place on the day it did. I usually tried to keep a tidy home, but I often fell short of "spotless." It was a simple coincidence that the night before I had taken time to thoroughly clean my home and set up Bobby's home schooling station exactly the way we wanted it. Bobby's desk was organized, clean and personal.

The social worker first spoke with Russell. That was the same semester that Russell was completing the seventh grade, and school would be starting within a half hour. Russell was asked if he was being fed enough, if he would show the social worker the inside of refrigerator, what type of shampoo he used, what type of activities he had after school, etc. Russell answered all the questions politely and was excused to go to school. A kiss good-bye and he was off.

When the social worker asked to see some of the homework Bobby was working on, we showed him a portfolio of his math, spelling, geography and art. I visited at length with the social worker that day. When he left, he told me that he intended to talk with his wife about the option of homeschooling their child. A few days later, I received a letter in the mail stating that the claim of child neglect was unsubstantiated

When I took Bobby out to homeschool for the last semester of his fourth grade year, I recognized a sort of alienation by his friends. He still played the same after-school games with the same group of neighborhood friends, but they started to distance themselves from him. Maybe it was due to having fewer things in common to talk about with them. Maybe it was due to the curious opinions passed along from parents who distrust change. Maybe Bobby seemed shy around those friends who constantly questioned his schooling situation.

The distance was very noticeable at the beginning of summer. When it was time for summer fun and games, Bobby was not called as quickly as he had been earlier in the year. He only noticed it. He didn't become obsessed or preoccupied with the observation. Eventually, by the middle the summer, everyone had pretty much forgotten the subject of school, and attitudes evened out.

I think when people are linked with family tradition, it is hard to break the traditions of those around them. People cling to the ideals of their parents. Sometimes when people do not have an opinion for themselves they adopt the opinion of their parents.

During that next summer, I received a letter from my ex-husband. It was a response to my request to modify our divorce decree and increase the amount of child support. For ten years, I had not acted on any prior legal advice to request an increase in the financial support from my ex-husband. However, our financial situation was not meeting the needs of the boys, and I could not earn enough with my part-time work to meet those increasing needs.

I knew that my ex-husband had re-married, had two more sons, and had moved on with his life. I also knew that his moving on did not include communication with his two firstborn sons. For the entire first ten years of the boys lives after the divorce, their father was in contact with them only four times.

I mention this to illustrate two points. First, the fact that the boys' physical needs were being met was something their father was oblivious to. I will say that he did abide the court-ordered payroll deduction. So he did, in fact, always pay the $150 per month per child. But $300 a month only met a fraction of the needs of those boys. I tried to make sure that their needs were taken care of. At times, our surroundings were meager to say the least.

The second reason I mention the lack of attention from the boys' father is to illustrate how often parents prioritize finances above the well-being of their children. As soon as I notified my ex-husband that I would be requesting that the courts allow an increase in child support, he immediately responded with accusations of neglect and abuse with regard to my homeschooling the boys. I thought it somewhat curious that someone who took so little interest in his children would take such exception to how they were being educated. He also threatened to seek a change in custody, stating that if I couldn't raise the boys on $300 per month, he would take the boys and do it himself.

By the middle of the summer, his attorney apparently told him that logically, if he thought he had a chance to change custody of the boys, he ought to at least make contact with them more often than four times per decade.

The boys did fly to Chicago for one week in the summer of 1992 to visit their father. So much time had elapsed since they had last seen their father that neither of them recognized him. The week was miserable for everyone. One of the things I had always made certain of was that schooling continued throughout the summer. I made sure that the boys took along their homeschooling workbooks and reading books. They both mentioned when they got home that their father encouraged them to relax and not spend so much time on school work. After all, "this was summer — nobody goes to school in the summer." However, the boys were bored and were happy to have something to spend their time on while in Chicago.

I think that the charges from my ex-husband claiming child abuse just because the boys were homeschooled were quickly dispelled. Spending one week with two boys that he didn't even know made everybody concerned miserable and canceled out any desire to ask the courts to change custody. Eventually, I was awarded an increase. We haven't heard from the father since. So much for his interest in the children — education and otherwise.

The next year Bobby was enrolled in fifth grade. He chose to go to school so he could stay close to his friends. Two things happened that year that were very un-nerving and were concerns worth mentioning.

During a unit of American history, some people came into Bobby's class to portray a reenactment of the civil war. In theory, this reenactment would have been a very interesting event. But the underlying message that Bobby picked up on was filled with intolerance and bigotry. The narrator was a member of a group made up of descendants of Southern officers of the Civil War. Bobby told me that the message he was picking up from the act was that the South should have won the Civil War and that there were still some deep-rooted hatred for people of color and distrust for anyone who was from the North. I was more than slightly concerned about the ideals and values that were being subtly passed along without the permission or the awareness of any of the parents.

When I asked the school if I could sit in on the next presentation, the reenactments were canceled.

The other concern I had was the constant fighting among the students within that particular classroom. Many times, Bobby would come home to tell me that the mood in his class resembled a mob mentality. When "the group" directed their anger, ridicule and/or antagonism to a particular student or couple of students, the effect was debilitating. The peer dependency that I witnessed in most of Bobby's classmates and beginning in Bobby was very disturbing. For the most part, Bobby was able to stay out of classroom conflicts, but on occasion he was swept up in the feeding frenzy of the classroom "group." A couple of times he was the object of the angry attention. After the mood would die down, and it always did after about three days, the "group" would find someone else to direct their anger to. That year Bobby noticed that "the group" decided what fashions to wear, which students were popular or dumb, what pastimes were in or out, etc.

I can say without hesitation that the year Bobby spent in fifth grade was the most disintegrating on his self esteem. Bobby went from being a happy, confident, friendly young man to being shy, hesitant and quiet. The change in Bobby's disposition was directly linked to his experience in a class in which the instructor completely neglected the need for training in cultural diversity and tolerance for differences. It took me a couple of years to help Bobby regain his confidence and self esteem. I learned a lot about the power of "the group" and the problems which result from negative peer pressure.

After Russell finished the seventh grade in public school, he began his eighth grade year in homeschool. Bobby continued in the fifth grade in public school. As I worked with Russell in his studies, I was convinced that he needed some supplemental classes. I knew that Russell could handle a foreign language class, a science class with a lab, and maybe a speech/drama class. I was aware that these classes were usually offered sometime in the junior and senior high school curriculums.

In some school districts there is a cooperative relationship between the public schools and homeschoolers. Often, homeschoolers can remain in the home for the core classes and attend public schools for activities, sports and specialty classes. I did approach the school district that the boys were in, but theirs was an all-or-nothing attendance policy. My next step was to call the closest junior college.

I was aware that in most public high schools, some of the honor students are allowed to leave school early on certain days to travel over to the local junior college to attend classes. By the time these honor students graduate from high school, many of them already have several hours of college credit since the high schools give high school requirement credit for the classes taken at junior colleges.

I began doing my homework on the idea of taking Russell to junior college twice a week so he could take advantage of the dual credit classes. I had seen several television news stories on children who attended colleges and universities. I sought out some of the students mentioned on these news programs. I located one particular 13-year-old boy in Oregon who was attending a university and was currently a junior in the school of engineering.

I spoke with the young man's mother at length about issues surrounding the sobering decision of putting a child in college. As it turns out, we had a lot in common. We had both recognized the potential of acceleration while our children were still quite young. We were both struggling single mothers. We were both determined not to let the bureaucracy of government deny our children what would be available to them if only they were older. Both of us had endured avalanches of criticism from well intentioned friends and family members regarding our decision to home school and then supplement our homeschooling with college-level classes. I gleaned a lot from this woman. I weighed the options and then decided to investigate the possibility of Russell attending the local Junior college part time.

After writing for and receiving a college catalog, I read the mission statement of the college. It stated that the college did not discriminate against age, sex, race, religion ... in its admission procedures. I became familiar with the admission requirements.

The requirements included a G.E.D. or a certificate of graduation from a recognized high school. Well, by that time, Russell was still too young to take the G.E.D test since a person can't even apply to take the test until the age of sixteen. However, at this point in time, I had a friend who was an instructor in the community education program and was in charge of teaching G.E.D. preparation classes to adults who wanted to earn their high school equivalence certificate. Within this program was a practice G.E.D. test which included sample questions similar to questions on an actual G.E.D exam.

I asked my friend if I could bring Russell in to take the practice test just to see which areas he would need improvement on when he finally did have the opportunity to take the exam. Everyone agreed that the results would be interesting, and Russell was excited to see if he was up to passing the test.

Russell took the practice test and passed every area with few mistakes. In some of the areas he made no mistakes, and his essay was graded and given an excellent rating. I had never put too much emphasis on standard test scores or class levels while the boys were in homeschool. We usually studied whatever was interesting to the boys, paying little attention to what age/grade level the subject was usually studied in the public schools.

I only paid attention to the minimum basic requirements of learning for their chronological age group just in case they ever needed to return to the public school. I never had much to worry about though. Both boys were usually ahead of the public school learning schedules. I understand that the advantages of homeschooling allow students to learn things quickly and then go on to learn more. Often homeschoolers are ahead of schedule whenever they have needed to return to the public school classrooms.

After it was confirmed to me that Russell could, in fact, pass the G.E.D. if he were ever given the opportunity to take it, I wanted to know how well he would do on a standard college acceptance test. The year before, when Russell was in seventh grade, he qualified to take the A.C.T. through the Duke Talent Search in the ALF class that he was attending. He had done well the year before, and I knew that he would probably do as well or even better now that he was a year older.

We sent off all the necessary forms, and Russell was soon scheduled to take the A.C.T. again this time without the Duke Talent Search. The test results came back, and Russell, at the age of eleven, had scored unusually high. Out of respect for his privacy, I won't give out his scores, but I will tell you the scores he received were all higher than the minimum required scores of an entering freshman to the local junior college.

I called the admissions office of Maple Woods Community College in Kansas City to confirm the procedures for the application process. I was informed that the college did, in fact, accept home school graduates and that a supplemental class could be approved for a homeschooler even before graduation. The requirements for admission for high school graduates included a composite score of at least seventeen on the A.C.T. and a certificate of completion from a recognized high school or a G.E.D certificate. The requirement for a high school supplemental class was simply a letter from the high school counselor recommending the student take the junior college courses. Russell could do that.

I knew that in the state of Missouri, at that time, the only thing needed for a student to graduate from high school, home or otherwise, was a letter of completion from the principal of that school. I was not only the counselor, but I was also the principal of Russell's high school.

When I told them how old Russell was (at that time he was eleven), a quick and absolute "no" was the answer to every possibility I questioned. When I asked the reason for the negative answers, Russell's age was given each and every time. When I asked about the nondiscrimination policy, I was quickly referred to the Dean of Students.

Mrs. Donetello was a former sixth grade teacher who had furthered her career to the level of Dean of Students for Maple Woods Community College. Since her prior experience had been with children of Russell's age group, it really didn't surprise me that she was not at all open to the idea of admitting a young child to a junior college. I knew that this was an extremely unusual request. I explained to her that I knew it seemed exceptional, but I also knew that Russell could academically handle the requested classes.

I tried to reassure her that I wasn't trying to introduce this child into the pressure-filled life of a full-time college student. I simply wanted to supplement his homeschooling with a few classes from the college. Russell needed some classes that I was not interested in nor prepared to teach. Still no cooperation.

Not only did Mrs. Donetello refuse to admit him, she refused to even interview him or review his application. When I reminded her of the college mission statement and threatened to go over her head to the Board of Trustees for an admission consideration, she finally agreed to interview Russell.

About a week after I spoke with Mrs. Donetello, I took Russell up to the junior college. We walked around the campus to get a good look at the buildings and classrooms. Russell seemed nervous but excited about being able take the more difficult classes of chemistry and French. I was still somewhat hesitant about Russell's ability to learn at this level.

Before Mrs. Donetello would agree to interview Russell, she required that he be given the college assessment test to gauge Russell's level of knowledge in basic math, English, Geography and science. I understood these tests are given to almost all students who enroll in college after attending homeschool, or who are returning college students when many years have passed since any formal classes had been taken, or students who enroll on academic probation. I knew that these tests serve a valuable purpose. The college enrollment counselors need to know where the student is academically so they can place the student at his or her academic level.

I had assumed that Russell would at least pass the remedial level and be placed in the first level of math and English. Much to my surprise, Russell's excitement and Mrs. Donetello's chagrin, Russell had scored high enough on each of the tests that he would be allowed to enroll in some of the intermediate level college classes, skipping the introductory classes most first-term freshmen start out with.

Mrs. Donetello was still not convinced. She insisted on seeing a portfolio of Russell's homeschool work, something no other qualifying freshman was required to do.

She also insisted that Russell schedule a session with the college psychologist. Again, something no other qualifying freshman was required to do.

She insisted that campus insurance policy prohibited admitting any student under the age of fourteen (although she never did produce a copy of the policy when I requested it). I assured her that I would accompany Russell everywhere he went on campus, even sit outside his classes while he attended.

After hours of conversations, Mrs. Donetello still refused to admit Russell to "her" college. Her reasons included her determination that Russell couldn't handle the academics, although the college's own assessment tests ruled that out. She insisted that Russell wouldn't be able to handle the social life, although he wasn't there for the social life, and that was not even an option I would allow. She insisted that Russell would miss out on his childhood. Although Russell's childhood was none of her business, I reassured her that I was making sure he didn't miss out on his childhood and argued that being interested in chemistry usually didn't automatically erase one's chances of a normal childhood.

After her final refusal to admit Russell, I wrote Mrs. Donetello a six-page letter. I reassured her that although I wanted to expose Russell to a level of learning higher than what she considered the norm, I would take great considerations to his childhood activities. He would continue to be in little league sports and boy scouts. He would continue to have friends his own age. He would continue to be active in the youth group at church.

I also suggested that she forward my request to her legal advisors because Russell met and/or exceeded every single requirement for admission to that junior college. As far as I could tell, the only reason for her not allowing Russell to attend was based on age discrimination. If that, in fact, was the case, I would file a lawsuit against her, and "her" school's Board of Trustees.

Within a week Russell was admitted on a one-term trial basis. We were told that the school needed to be convinced that Russell could handle the classroom pressure and the academic requirements. Mrs. Donetello insisted that Russell only take one three-hour class his first semester. However, I knew that the minimum class load to receive the financial aid of the Pell Grant was at least six hours per term. I also knew that my finances were stretched as far as they could go. I needed the grant's help if Russell was going to enroll. So Russell enrolled in six semester hours (two classes, three times per week) and attended Maple Woods Community College beginning January 1993.

CHAPTER EIGHT: *First Term Freshman*

I remember vividly the first day I drove Russell to college. I remember thinking that his tests scores indicated his advanced intelligence. But the small stature of this little person reminded me that Russell had just turned twelve years old. It was a very sobering thing that I was doing. It was not something that I was taking lightly. I was acutely aware of the stress and the expectations Russell may have been under.

As we drove the fifty-minute route to the junior college that first week in January, I remained very careful about the conversation with my son. I wanted to pick up any hesitation from him about going to college. I started the conversation by asking Russell how he was feeling about his first day of school. His answer surprised me.

He told me that he was not sure that he was smart enough to go to college since he didn't go through all the classes most high school students go through. He told me that he didn't think he knew all the things he needed to know to take the classes he was enrolled in.

We talked for a while, and I told him that anytime — ANYTIME WHATSOEVER — he wanted to quit, he just needed to say the word. I would pull him out without asking any questions. I reminded him that the reason he was going to classes was to learn more. People don't go to college because they know everything already. People go to college to learn things they don't already know. Russell thought about that for awhile. He smiled and then seemed ready to go.

I walked Russell to class that day and kissed his cheek. I waited for him to finish, and when he came out of that classroom, I was very relieved to see how happy and excited he was. I questioned him, and on the way home Russell and I were both satisfied that he was up to the challenge of those two classes in that junior college.

I had decided that if I was going to drive Russell to class every day and stay on campus with him, I might as well take a class or two myself. I enrolled that semester in a couple of classes which were scheduled straight down the hall from Russell's classes. At the end of every class, we would meet and either go to the library to study until the next class, or we drove home and studied until Bobby came home from his fifth grade class in public school.

During the first couple of weeks of Russell's college attendance, many teachers were caught off guard. One of his teachers later told me that when he first saw Russell sitting in class, he just concluded that Russell was a child of a student.

Sometimes older adult students brought their children to class to sit quietly and study, read or color until the parent was finished with the one class. This practice was frowned upon by teachers and administrators. But it did happen on occasion, especially on days when the public elementary schools had parent-teacher conferences, snow days or scheduled days off. It wasn't until the third or fourth day of teaching this class that the instructor realized that Russell was, in fact, a student.

Russell did well that semester and adjusted quickly to the structure of college classes. He actually didn't enroll in the classes we had intended for him to take when we first investigated the possibility of supplementing his homeschooling with college classes. He ended up enrolling in an English composition class and in a public speaking class.

That first experience with college during the spring term of 1993 was exceptional. Russell learned quite a bit about how things ran outside the confines of a public elementary school.

The subjects were presented in an adult manner. The English class instructor chose the book *One Flew over the Cuckoo's Nest* for the class reading assignments. This book was a bit controversial for Russell, but it did give him a perspective on people that he had never considered to this point. Reading this book prepared him to handle viewpoints that were not consistent with his own. We were able to talk personally and discuss the content and the reasoning behind our opinions about the story and the characters. It was definitely a book that would not have been read by most children his age, but Russell was responding to what he was reading and to his classroom discussions with a logic and understanding that most children his age didn't seem to possess.

Also in his English class, Russell had to keep a daily journal about his reading. Half the grade for the class depended on that journal. Although some of his fellow students shrugged off the assignment, Russell tried to do the assignments as they were outlined in the class syllabus. He began to notice that some of the other students were not taking their assignments as seriously. I was glad that Russell got to see how some of the other students would skip class, ignore their assignments and complain about tests. Although he usually tried to keep up with the class load, Russell was able to witness the consequences of a situation that was totally the responsibility of the student.

He found out that if the student does not do his homework, no letters go home to Mom. If the student misses a test, he isn't sent to the principal's office. Nobody is responsible for the student's performance except the student.

I tried to take the opportunity to teach Russell that this is exactly the way it is in life. Every single able-bodied human being is responsible for a set amount of duties. If those things don't get accomplished, the consequences are personal and individual. Just as a student will receive the grade which reflects his effort and ability, a person will achieve their goals in life as a reflection of his efforts and abilities.

Russell was able to keep up with the two initial classes that semester. By the time the semester ended and the grades were received, Russell felt very good about his efforts. He received an A and a B. Since the classes that Russell took the first semester went so smoothly, he decided to try another semester. So we started to plan what he should take the next semester.

The next term was summer. Going to summer school was not foreign to the boys because I always had them continue with their workbooks and reading programs during the summers. Russell was agreeable, so he decided that he would enroll in an algebra class and another English class.

We also decided to fill out more applications for continued financial aid. Along with the regular Pell Grant application, there was an application for a small amount of money available based on prior academic performance. Russell qualified, and he was offered a small scholarship based on his grades from the previous term. However, someone didn't tell the enrollment office that they were offering Russell that grade-based scholarship.

When we went to the enrollment counter to sign him up for summer classes, we found that there was a "hold" on his records. Apparently the staff had been instructed by Mrs. Donetello that Russell was not allowed further enrollment. I tried to speak with her, but "her schedule was quite full." The first day of summer classes was approaching, and Russell's enrollment was still on hold, and I still had not been able to speak with Mrs. Donetello. Finally, after calling several times one day and leaving messages each time, she returned my call.

I asked her why the "hold" had been place on Russell's enrollment. She told me that she thought she had made herself perfectly clear, that Russell would only be allowed to attend one semester to take some home school supplemental classes. After that I would need to find another avenue.

Her reaction didn't make sense to me. First, that was not the agreement. The agreement was that Russell would be allowed to enroll in two classes the first semester on a trial basis. Since Russell performed so well during that first semester both socially and academically, and since her own financial aid office offered him a performance scholarship, I could hardly see what her complaint about future enrollment was. Second, Russell was not even allowed to take the classes we initially wanted to enroll him in due to Mrs. Donetello's restrictions. Instead, he enrolled in two classes that were acceptable to both Mrs. Donetello and Russell, so he didn't have to start out with seemingly difficult classes.

Still, Mrs. Donetello insisted that she had the right as the Dean of Students to deny Russell future enrollment. So, once again I wrote to Mrs. Donetello, stating that Russell would like to accept the scholarship that the college offered him, explaining which classes Russell wanted to enroll in, and the reasons why he wanted to enroll in them. Once again, I tried to reassure her that I was not going to let my son endure more academic pressure than he was capable of handling and that he would be watched very carefully for signs of stress or fatigue. I also reminded her that Russell had performed as well or better than the average freshman in "her" college and that there was no logical reason for her denying him enrollment. If she did not allow Russell to enroll that semester and did not provide any concrete legal reasoning as to why or why not, I would file a lawsuit against her and "her" school for age discrimination. I carbon copied the letter to the president of the college. Russell enrolled the next week.

This term was also a great semester. It was a summer term, so the classes were not as crowded as the previous term. Russell seemed to do well and seemed happy with the classes he was taking. This term Bobby would ride with us as I drove Russell to class. While Russell was in class, Bobby and I worked on workbooks for him. We were all happy to have lots of time left over each day for doing summer things. The boys played little league baseball, went swimming, camping and stayed up late on Friday nights watching double features at the drive-in movies. Classes were held only four times a week, so on Fridays both boys usually slept in and I was able to catch up on some contract piece-work to keep some income.

The big thing that happened during the summer of 1993 was the 500-Year-Flood that affected the entire Midwestern states of the Mississippi valley. We had spent quite a bit of time that summer helping the town sandbag to protect the levees surrounding the farms.

Russell was nearing finals when the National Guard came to our home and told us that we had one hour to gather our things and move to higher ground. With the help of church members, we were able to pack nearly everything we owned into several trucks, cars and vans of friends who had come to help. We walked out of the front door as water was beginning to creep into the living room.

CHAPTER NINE: *After the Flood*

Two days after we were evacuated, I drove back to the area to survey the damage. The entire town was covered with water. Traffic was stopped outside the city about a half a mile. Nobody was allowed inside the national guard boundaries. The only things visible were the rooftops of homes and businesses and tall trees.

This had been the third time we had been evacuated. The first two times were precautions, and we were allowed to move back in within a few days. But the third time we were forced out, the damage was so extensive that we had to find a place to move into permanently.

After the move back into the city, Russell transferred colleges to an affiliate of the junior college where he first enrolled. Longview Community College had the same core requirements and offerings for an associates degree as Maple Woods Community College. For this term, Russell enrolled in four classes which was considered full time.

The administration of Longview Community College did seem somewhat hesitant when Russell went to enroll, but nobody at this school acted as if they were unhappy that he was there. The Dean of Students, Dr. Fred Grogan, was certainly supportive and encouraging. He offered Russell help with any questions and hoped that Russell would come to him if he ever needed the help of an administrator. He checked on Russell's progress and adaptability often and made sure Russell was happy with the way he was being treated and with the things he was learning.

The classes that Russell enrolled in that fall included geography and philosophy. During this same semester Russell came down with a severe case of chicken pox. His Geography instructor refused to let him make up any missed work, stating that it was his policy not to excuse *any* absences. When Russell explained that he certainly did not want to expose all those adult men to a potentially damaging disease, his instructor refused to believe him. "Chicken pox is a childhood disease," he stated. Russell informed him that indeed he was still a child. This instructor had not noticed the small student sitting in the middle of his classroom and Russell's grades and classroom participation seemed to blend in well enough that he never brought attention to himself. Still, the instructor didn't let Russell make up any of the missed work. As a result, Russell received a C grade in Geography.

During this same semester, Russell completed a philosophy class. I had some reservations about his taking this class because of the overview of many "Godless" religions and theories. I had worked relentlessly to instill a faith in God in both my sons. I was hesitant about a class that could turn his belief and faith around in a short term of school.

I spoke at length with Russell about the concern I had with this class. I told him to keep his resolve. But I also told him to study the philosophy of other religions to find out what parts he agreed with and what parts he did not. I hoped that by studying other philosophies he could develop an understanding and acceptance of others' beliefs just as he wants others to have an acceptance of his beliefs.

Russell studied and passed with a good grade and seemed to hold on to the things I had taught him. I was happy to have him experience this class because I know that he will be presented with lots of challenges to his beliefs during his life both inside and outside the classroom.

This same term, Bobby decided to try the middle school in the new town. By now Bobby was in the sixth grade. At the beginning of the semester, he was very happy with everything. He liked most of his teachers and was glad to be involved in classes he knew I wouldn't be offering in homeschool (team sports, group music, etc.)

By mid-October, however, Bobby wanted to come home. He tired easily of the slamming lockers, the vulgar language of the kids, the pushing and shoving in the hallways as the students rushed from class to class in the too-few minutes provided. I brought Bobby home and homeschooled him for the rest of that semester and the next semester.

The next semester was spring. During that semester, Russell was invited to continue his scholarship for being on the President's Honor Roll, and he also was invited to be inducted as one of the youngest members of a national honors association for America's junior colleges, Phi Theta Kappa.

The organization hosted honors seminars, guest speakers for the college, service projects, fund raisers, etc. This was a great organization for him to belong to. The addition of this club to his schedule made his social exposure quite extensive.

Both boys were active in little league sports on town teams. They were both active with their peers in the young men's programs at church. They were very active with the Boy Scouts of America. They had plenty of friends their own age, and now Russell was active with a group of students whose ages ranged from 13 (himself) to 47 (an older student who had lost his job and was now in the retraining program at the community college).

I think that one advantage Russell and Bobby have over their peers is that they had the opportunity to develop communication skills and interests in people other than those limited to their own age group. This advantage has helped them in their college activities, and I think it will continue to help them as their lives go on.

One fun story I like telling about this semester happened on Easter Friday. The student body of a community college is made up differently from that of a university. The average age of the student body is older than the average age of most four-year schools. There are plenty of teens who have just graduated from high school, but there are several other age groups as well. Many displaced workers who need retraining because of layoffs or injuries will attend, as well as many displaced homemakers who suddenly find themselves single heads of households. There are also plenty of older adults who simply want to increase their chances for advancement by increasing their education and college credentials by returning to college part-time while working full-time. Whatever the cases were, Russell was surrounded by a student body made up of older students.

On the Thursday before Easter, the student government passed out notices about an Easter egg hunt to be held the next day. Early Friday morning before the sun was even up, members of the student government were out hiding eggs. It was pretty obvious that not many students paid attention to the handouts and flyers, because the next day it seemed that nobody was hunting for the Easter eggs.

Since it seemed age-appropriate that Russell hunted for the eggs, he went for it. He found that the eggs were filled with candy, tokens to the student canteen and, in some cases, money. At first, Russell was running through the lawns and hallways of campus filling his backpack with eggs as the older adoring students watched and smiled at how cute he was.

Then, as Russell began to find more and more of the eggs containing money, he would encourage those who were watching him to find some for themselves. Some older students did join him, and soon someone shouted, "Hey, there's fifty dollars in here!" It didn't take long for Russell to be joined on his Easter egg hunt by hundreds of older adult students looking of the pastel plastic eggs. It was a fun day, and it was fun to see all those "kids" looking for the eggs. Maybe Russell wasn't too far from his peer group after all.

The next term was summer. Russell wanted to take a Karate class. Bobby wanted to also. So I called the college and told them that I was homeschooling Russell's little brother just as I had Russell and I wondered if Bobby could enroll along with Russell in this Karate class. Dean Grogan interviewed Bobby, examined his records, saw that he had also done well on the A.C.T. and allowed him to enroll on a part-time status in the Karate class.

Although their instructor liked having two students of the same size for sparring sessions, he didn't give either of the boys an advantage in their performance strictly because of their ages or their sizes. They both did well and enjoyed the class.

The following term was Russell's last term before graduating with an Associates Degree. Since Bobby was now on the computer listed as a current student, he didn't have to go through the same first-time enrollment hassles that Russell did. We simply went down to the registration office and enrolled him into a couple of classes to supplement his home school. That semester Bobby took public speaking and history.

The day Russell graduated from Longview Community College was a great day in my life. I can only compare it to what a parent would feel at the graduation of their children from high school. I knew Russell worked hard at achieving his degree, and he looked very happy and proud.

Russell wore a sash around his shoulders to indicate that he was graduating with honors as a member of Phi Theta Kappa. We both knew that Russell's graduating from a junior college was not the end of his schooling, but it did give Russell a huge sense of accomplishment.

During the few week before Russell graduated from Longview, I spent time researching the possible four-year colleges for Russell to transfer to. I would drive both boys to classes and then go to the library to read through the various college catalogs of the colleges and universities in the area.

After narrowing the colleges down to three, I took the boys to the three campuses to tour and meet the advisors. We put a lot of thought into which college to transfer to. It wasn't so much an individual decision as it was a family decision, because wherever Russell went, so did his little brother. And, if it meant the family moved so the boys could go to college, wherever they went, so did I. It meant that I would need to relocated the entire family, find other part-time employment, find a place to live, etc.

We decided to have Russell finish his four-year degree at Central Missouri State University in Warrensburg, Missouri. After finding a nice little apartment for us to live in, I found a job at a local bakery. I had been decorating cakes for many years by then, and even though it is not something I like having to do to support my family, I knew I could decorate until a more suitable job developed.

A more suitable job did develop, and I began working as a secretary at CMSU. I felt that this job was the most convenient for the whole family. I was on campus for the boys. If at any time they should ever need me, I was close. The apartment I found was only about six blocks from school, so the boys could walk back and forth on their own. The pay and benefit package at my new job was good enough for me to want to stay until the boys were finished. At that time, there was a slight discount for students whose parents worked at the school.

A lot of fun things happened while the boys attended CMSU. They both liked the freedom of having school so close to where we lived. Up to this point, their commute was about an hour each way. This is the term Russell got his first job. He was hired as a computer lab assistant to check students into the computer lab. They both liked having classes that they were interested in and loved the computer labs. And this is the term that they discovered the internet. Bobby was hooked. At the time of this writing, Bobby is currently working at an internet provider.

The time seemed to move quickly at CMSU. Soon I realized that Russell would be graduating, and he was still too young to enter the job market. So we began to talk about what he wanted to do when he was finished at CMSU. He had always discussed the possibility of his going to law school. We discussed the things he had to do to be considered for law school, and he decided he wanted to go for it.

During the last semester of his junior year, Russell registered to take the LSAT (Law School Aptitude Test). He did well enough to qualify for acceptance at many of the major colleges in the nation.

We started to investigate the possibility of law school. I was hesitant about sending someone so young to graduate school. I talk more about how I arrived at the conclusion to allow Russell to go to Law School in chapter eleven. However, when all the options were completely investigated, Russell ended up being accepted at the Missouri University School of Law.

Bobby, now in his sophomore year, transferred to M.U. along with Russell so we could all stay together as a family while the boys went to college. I sometimes felt a little bad for Bobby. I know that most of the attention as to what school they should attend surrounded Russell. But each time they transferred, Bobby fit right into the classes and the new campus.

I remember being with Bobby on the day he took his driver's license test after he turned sixteen. By now he was a junior at M.U. majoring in computer science. He told me he was glad that he came to M.U. and that he thought the school was really working out for him. This gave me a great deal of comfort.

CHAPTER TEN:
Some Thoughts about Homeschooling

I am going to dedicate this chapter to describing some of my observations about the past fifteen years. I have developed many strong opinions about homeschooling and people's reaction to me as a homeschooler. Usually these reactions are the outcome of the direction I have taken towards my children's education.

I continue to get comments about robbing my children of their childhood. Most of the time when I hear this comment I become incensed. I am always amazed that someone who knows nothing about how much effort I put into making sure the boys were exposed to age-appropriate activities and to friends their own ages can make such a comment. I usually do not go around jumping to conclusions and making comments about the deficits in other parent's choices. Yet so often people will make a judgment call about how normal my children are or are not without even having a chance to meet them. I think the tendency to jump to these conclusions is snobbish and presumptuous.

Making judgmental comments about issues when one does not see the entire picture reeks of ignorance. So people who do this are simply ignorant. These same observant adults would never (or should never) accept bigoted and misinformed comments about their own "well-trained, public-schooled" children.

Another comment I constantly endure is one about putting too much pressure on my children. Well, let's see. Both my children have no more than three classes per day, and they only take classes which interest them. They spend hours studying things they will use in their careers, and they are surrounded by interesting people from all races, ages and lifestyles.

To me their situation does not seem very pressure-packed. On the other hand, trying to concentrate on up to seven different classes each day, having homework in most of them, having after-school activities and maybe a part-time job as well as trying to maintain a social life acceptable to one's peers does seem pressure-packed. My children, although acutely aware of their class load and responsibilities, are in no way trying to handle more than what would normally be considered acceptable.

I get a huge kick out of the way many people downgrade the accomplishments the boys have made and the way they have made them. Many people have mentioned that their children could have done the same thing (meaning attending college at a younger age) if they had allowed it. I sometimes get the sense that many parents who are justifiably proud of their children turn the whole education issue into a contest. I am the first one to agree that many children could learn things faster and advance at a quicker pace than the average school curriculums allows. But it isn't a race.

The fact that the boys took the educational avenues that they did does not mean that I am trying to convince anyone that they should follow suit. I have taken plenty of criticism and endured comments such as, "Well, eventually the children who attend public schools will be in college, and they will catch up to your kids. Then everybody will be even." That is probably true. Although again, I do not consider the education of my children a contest. The fact that they will complete their education sooner does not necessarily mean they are better people. It is not a contest and it never was meant to be.

I have also observed people's reaction when they find out the boys are socially very normal and emotionally are right on the "normal" scale. I am reminded of one particular time when Russell was in the seventh grade. He was with a group of older students who were being disruptive and rowdy during a school-sponsored outing. They were all called on to calm down. When the instructor reached Russell, her response was, "I expected more out of *you*." Why? I thought to myself, "Now wait a minute, you can't have it both ways. You can't complain about my robbing him of his childhood and in the same breath complain that Russell was acting in an immature manner." He was acting his age, for heaven's sake. Yes, both the boys study out of books which contain a higher lever of instruction than the books their chronological peers study from. But they both enjoy being socially and emotionally the age they are.

I have endured comments that imply any misbehavior from the boys is directly due to the fact that they did not have the normal exposure to regular schools. Hum. Does this mean that the children who attend public schools and who complete the levels of classroom studies normally offered are free from any behavior problems? I don't think so. In fact, I have spoken to plenty of families who have removed their children from public schools specifically **because** the misbehavior of some of the other (*regularly trained*) students have disrupted the lives of their children and their ability to learn.

I am amused at the reaction of some adults who find out that the boys are educationally accelerated and attempt to have a very "adult" conversation with them. One of our neighbors who worked as a financial advisor told me that he wanted to "pick Russell's brain" about some investment possibilities. Russell may have seemed a little rude, but he just shrugged. He didn't want to talk about investments; he wanted to go watch *Animaniacs* on TV.

I remember one professor at a college that we were touring when we were deciding on a four-year college for the boys. After meeting this "prodigy," he went into his office and came back with a 500-page book and handed it to Russell. "I think you will find this very interesting." It was a book about logarithms. Russell and Bobby spent their free time reading about baseball cards and video games, not about logarithms.

Some adults seem disappointed with the fact that just because the boys were able to learn things quickly did not also mean they were interested in doing so. One time at a Boy Scout meeting, a leader was talking about pumice and the reason pumice was important. He started grilling Bobby and was surprised that Bobby not only did not know very much about geology, neither did he care about it.

Maybe one day Bobby will care about pumice and geology. And maybe one day Russell will care about logarithms and investments. But for now, they want to study subjects that interest them. And for now, their hobbies and interests are very age-appropriate.

Something that always bothered some of the adults who were aware of the boys' educational situation was the fact that neither one of them were interested in making the Dean's list each and every term. It isn't important to them or to me that they are at the top of their classes. Russell had been able to maintain an above average grade in most of his classes. But Bobby is more like me when it comes to studying — all or nothing.

When I was a student, I excelled and worked hard in the subjects that interested me. And in the subjects that didn't I either failed or received a below average grade. Bobby does not have a 4.0 grade point average in all of his classes, but neither do most students who attend college. That is why honor students are called *honor students.* Because they excel above the average. Does this mean that the average student has no merit? No, it means the average student is *average.* Without average students, honor students would not have anyone left to be compared to except failing students. Luckily, in most colleges, it is not an all-or-nothing grading scale. There are some honor students. There are some failing students. And then there are quite a few students who fall somewhere in the middle. I have noticed that somewhere in the middle is where Bobby and I fit most comfortably.

I have also had to deal with people who were under the misconception that I had some secret answer to their children's educational problems. I remember when Russell started his first semester in college. The novelty of a twelve-year-old attending classes at a college was quite the story. TV stations and newspaper articles carried the story for a while. Russell and I were both glad when the attention settled down.

Some people, however, wanted to do the same thing with their children. I was caught off guard when some parents asked me for help. I didn't know their children. I wasn't convinced that their children were in the same situation as Russell and Bobby. So when I declined to advise them as to how they too could get their kids into college by age twelve, I received quite a few negative reactions.

Although I do think that more children could take advantage of the opportunities available and investigate other avenues of education, I do not consider our situation as some sort of model that should be followed. If a child is happy and doing well in public school, and the parents of that child are happy about all the advantages to their child being in that school, then I don't see any reason to make a change. However, if children or their parents are not happy with public school and a change needs to be made, I am stating that there are plenty of alternatives. We simply chose a very unusual path to take.

When I encountered several parents who had problems with their children's behavior, I was completely at a loss as to what to advise. I talked with one mother whose son was so bored with school that he was beginning to become a behavioral problem for his teacher. After speaking with me, his mother pulled him out of school. She taught him herself, and for the classes she did not feel competent to teach she hired a tutor. The change in his behavior was remarkable. He returned to being the happy, loving, interested boy his mother had once known. He completed his G.E.D. when he was old enough and began a job in a machinist shop. Everyone is happy.

I spoke to another mother, however, who was certain that her son was causing trouble at school because he was a genius. Well, I've heard of bad behavior being a result of boredom, but this young man had a lengthy police record. I could not help this woman no matter how much she thought our children's situation were similar. In fact, it scared me to think that her decision about her son's future rested on my advice to her.

I had accepted a couple of jobs tutoring some children while my sons were both at the junior college. Although I was the same teacher who substituted for the local elementary school a term earlier, the newspaper stories that ran made my teaching abilities seem stronger than they were before the stories ran.

One of the little boys I tutored benefited greatly from the one-on-one homework sessions. He was a delight to be with and the parents were both supportive. Neither his parents nor I pretended that my tutoring him was anything more than what the mother would be doing if she was able to get off work earlier. Her work took her out of town, and by the time she got home her son was simply not interested or too tired to study more. I was hired to pick him up from school and start right in with him on his homework. He worked well with me and his grades improved. No magic — just some assertive attention. Then when his mother got home, they were able to enjoy each other without the battle of homework.

I was also hired to tutor another young boy in that same grade. I knew immediately that there was a problem with this boy's ability to learn. I felt very inadequate and advised the parents to take him to professionals. The mother, however, would not hear of the possibility that anything could be *wrong* (her words, not mine) with her son. I tutored him for only a few weeks and then told the mother that I couldn't help. Later the young man was diagnosed with autism.

The fact is, some students need the professional help that only the schools can give. Some children need the speech therapy that is offered through the school systems. Some children need the attention of teachers who are trained in special education. There are some students who, although the parents would like to homeschool, just will not sit and learn from their own parents.

I tell these stories because I know that many people want answers to problems with their children's schooling questions. Even though Russell and Bobby seem somewhat advantaged, the direction they took may or may not be the same one other students need to take. I am the first to champion alternatives, however.

There was a time when I was able to help a family with their young teen-age daughter, though. This particular girl was losing self-esteem quickly, and depression was starting to set in. The family had taken the girl to counseling and was on top of her depression. However, the problems at school slowed her healing. This particular girl was a victim of sexual harassment by several of the other students — amazingly both boys *and* girls. The girl had developed physically much faster than her peers and was being chided at school for the size of her chest. "Marilyn Monroe" and "Miss Double-D" were names she had become known by. Intelligent life would see this as a big problem, but the school officials didn't take the family's concerns seriously. The teasing continued and so did the decline of the girl's self esteem.

The parents came to me in tears and begged for help. They didn't expect me to make their average-grade daughter into an honor student. They only needed guidance in setting up a homeschool for their daughter. I was able to teach the parents how to conduct a home school. I let them in on the minimum state requirements for a homeschool and told them what they needed to accomplish so that the state would recognize their lessons as meeting the basic minimum requirements for her grade level.

And one more thing that I was able to do. I put together a lesson plan for the rest of the year which included seven subjects in workbooks which they could purchase from a nearby teachers' supply store. I assured them that there were advantages and disadvantages of the decision they were making. The family was nervous about taking their daughter out of a once friendly school and teaching her at home. But they told me they were willing to try anything to get this girl back to the happy, fun daughter they once had.

It worked. By the end of that term she was completing her assignments early each day so she could spend more time doing the things she loved — crafts and reading. We moved the following summer so I never knew what became of the young girl. But, I am sure that for one spring semester of her life she felt confident and secure around the people she loved and who loved her enough to make a drastic change in their lives.

There were several parents who wanted to hire me because their children suffered from Attention Deficit Disorder. Most of the time the disorder had not been diagnosed, but the parents were certain that their child suffered from it. Well, let's see. Both parents work 40 to 50 hours per week. They hire their housekeeping done. They go out to eat because they do not have time to cook. They pay for camps for the summer and send their children to sitters on school breaks. There actually may be a case of attention deficit — just not on the part of the student.

Now, I am not stating that it is wrong for both parents to work. Most people fall into that category. I can think of many, many families with two working parents that are enormously successful in paying attention to their children. Neither am I stating that activities for the summer are not worthwhile. But I am stating that some parents want to hire their problems out to subcontractors and think they are acting in the best interest of the child.

Just as there are plenty of reasons to homeschool children, there are just as many reasons not to. I am thinking of one group of homeschooling families who homeschool purely out of social defiance. The whole attitude of "nobody and/or no government is going to tell me what I can or cannot do with my kid" is quickly apparent.

I am acutely familiar with the hysterical conservative movement which thinks that anything that goes wrong in their lives is directly linked to a satan-contolled government conspiracy. I think the only benefits to families of socially defiant homeschoolers are to the paranoid egos of the parents. The children certainly do not benefit, and neither does the society that has to absorb them once their parents are finished with them. I have personally met several families who fall into this group.

These children are socially handicapped, and some of them can't read well enough to even complete a job application. Some of these homeschooled children would not be able to pass a basic minimum skills test nor the G.E.D. What these families are doing to their own children borders on neglect.

The children of these families are suffering because of the fanatic attitude of their parents. I have encountered many families like the ones I've just described, and for the most part I refuse to even get into a conversation with them. The disservice they continue to do to their own children and to their community is disgusting to me. I do not even like being considered a homeschooler when people such as these are considered in the same category.

CHAPTER ELEVEN: *Answered Prayers*

I am going to dedicate this chapter to a spiritual angle. If you are not interested in the spiritual aspect of our story, go on to the epilogue.

During the last fifteen years, I spent quite a bit of time on my knees in prayer. I did not take lightly my mantle of motherhood. Neither did I think I was capable of making decisions of great magnitude on my own. I owe all of the success I have had with my family to divine intervention. I have a deep-rooted belief in the power of prayer.

Each time I was faced with making a decision which affected my two sons, I took the matter to the Lord in prayer. Most of the miracles that have happened in my life are so personal that I don't really wish to print them and put them up for public scrutiny. But I do have a couple of stories that I would like to share.

I was about to let Russell take the LSAT exam. I knew that he would soon be graduating from CMSU, and I was not sure exactly what he should do next. Bobby and I were doing just fine where we were. I had a job that paid well, and Bobby was happy and doing well in school. I knew that if Russell was admitted to law school it meant another move for our family.

I remember praying to the Lord and telling him that I needed help with this decision. I didn't want to move. I liked our lives just the way they were. I needed to know the direction I should take with Russell's education. And I needed to know beyond a shadow of a doubt. So that night I began a fast. As I prayed, I told the Lord that I was fasting so the results of Russell's test would unmistakably point us in the right direction.

The next day I drove Russell over to the building at the university where the testing was being conducted. The test would last four hours. I went back home and continued to concentrate on the results of the test. I prayed every hour and pleaded with the Lord that if Russell was intended to go to law school, he would do well on the test. If

Russell was not intended to go to law school, I would know which direction to take.

When I picked Russell up from the test that rainy Saturday in September, I asked him how he felt about the test. He told me that he felt really good and that he was ready for the results whatever they might be. He seemed tired but happy that the test was over.

It took weeks for the test results to return. I knew what scores were needed for Russell to even be considered for admission to a law school. To be considered for admission to University of Missouri at Kansas City he needed to have a score of at least 150 in addition to other admission criteria. To be considered for admission to M.U. he needed a 155. To be considered for admission to Yale or Harvard (not that those schools were ever considerations) he needed a score of 160. I won't tell you the exact score, but I will tell you that when the results finally arrived, his scores were well above all the minimum required scores for any of the schools Russell was considering.

It should have seemed that I had my answer, but I still wasn't convinced. I started calling different law schools to see what their admission requirements were. It seemed that Russell qualified for several schools. We finally decided to check out Missouri University. M.U. rated high among the nation's law schools in student satisfaction and was still close to home. I called the school and scheduled a visit.

My next day of fasting and prayer was the day Russell filled out the admission application. I prayed that if, in fact, Russell was intended to go to law school, he would be accepted to the only college he applied to. And if Russell was not intended to go to law school, he would not be accepted but he would feel good about the direction that he did take.

Within a couple of weeks Russell received a letter of acceptance to Missouri University School of Law.

I'm not sure why I was so hesitant about letting Russell go to law school. But I was still not convinced that he was really supposed to go.

I had signed a lease for the home we were renting and knew that if I did not complete the term of the lease, I would still be held financially responsible for the full amount. I had talked with the rental managers about getting out of the lease with a thirty-day notice, and they insisted that I would be held to the full term of the lease.

Even though all of my other prayers had been answered, I needed to know that what I was doing was in accordance to the plan that the Lord had for both Russell and Bobby. Once again, I fasted and prayed. I prayed that if I was to pack up my family and move to Columbia, Missouri, so that my sons could attend M.U., a way would be made for me to get out of my lease.

Within a week, I received notice that the home I was renting had been sold and that I was released from my lease. I figured it was time for us to pack.

I told Russell that we would be moving to Columbia so that he and Bobby could both attend M.U. A few weeks later, the three of us drove to Columbia to tour the campus, to meet with some of the advisors, to fill out job applications and to check out family housing.

The day was splendid. All of the people we spoke with were encouraging and friendly. I found out the campus did have many employment opportunities for me. Bobby was happy about the computer science program M.U. offered. Finally, that day we looked at campus housing for family living.

I remember standing inside the apartment wondering if I was doing the right thing for my sons. I remember looking through the window at the two of them standing outside next to the car talking intently to each other. I had insisted that they should wear their church clothes for the tours to show respect for their advisors. I remember thinking how grown up they both looked. Were my little boys growing up too fast? Was I robbing them of their childhood? When I walked back out to the car, I heard what the two of them had been discussing. They were arguing about whose turn it was to sit in the front seat. I had my answers.

After we moved to Columbia, I began to ponder the realization that soon the boys would have lives of their own and that my job as guardian would finish. We were all sharing a small apartment on campus, and the situation had become one more of roommates rather than guardian and children. We were cramped, but for the most part happy.

That August, Russell started law school, Bobby transferred in computer science, and I took a job at a local bank. I was noticing that the boys were handling this college experience very well. Our lives were speeding by, and the boys seemed happy and healthy. I could not stop wondering what the Lord had in store for me once my boys were on their own.

In November, I was asked to be the director of the Christmas program at our church. I worked hard at scripting out a play which would follow a dinner. Things were going smoothly with the rehearsals. But a week before the last dress rehearsal, my narrator informed me that she was going to have to drop out. Where was I going to find a narrator at this late date?

I remember sitting in choir practice on that Sunday afternoon looking at all the choir members trying to decide which of those available would make a good narrator for the impending Christmas program. I looked at the bass section and saw a man whom I had not yet met. I asked the woman sitting next to me who he was. She said his name was Richard Seibert. After choir practice, I walked up to Richard and introduced myself. I told him about my dilemma, and he graciously accepted the assignment of narrator.

During the rehearsals and set-up activities for the Christmas program, I had a chance to get to know Richard a little better. It turned out we had a lot in common. We both like to sing, we both love being active in service projects, and we both loved learning about new things in life.

The Christmas program went off without a hitch. The following May I married Richard. Someone could say that the answers to the prayers I was offering were merely a string of coincidences. But I say that the things that happened to lead up to Russell's acceptance to law school had to happen so I would be convinced to move to a city where my future husband would be waiting. After being a single head of household for fifteen years, I didn't need to worry about what I was going to do with my life once the boys were on there own. I would be spending it with my husband — the answer to a secret prayer.

EPILOGUE

So here we are. Russell will graduate law school by the time he is eighteen. Bobby thinks he may take a couple of years off to work for a computer firm. Both boys have been at Missouri University for two years now. At the beginning of their first semester, I suggested that they keep a journal of their time at M.U. Maybe they will write a sequel to this book to let those interested know how their lives have progressed several years from now.

During the first semester at M.U., both Russell and Bobby obtained part-time jobs. Russell worked at the law school computer lab as a computer assistant. He also accepted a part-time job with a law professor as a research clerk. During the summer between his first two years of law school, Russell worked as a clerk for a criminal attorney. His experience there was invaluable. The things he learned that summer will help him both as a future attorney and as a responsible employee.

Bobby put his computer knowledge to work and accepted a part-time position with one of the local banks as a web-site programmer. By "surfing" the internet, he was able to secure many free-lance assignments to write computer programs for private companies and individuals. He presently works as an information specialist for an internet provider. He has developed a program which will enable computer security companies to program more accurately, quickly and efficiently. He has contacted a patent attorney to secure his program.

During their time at M.U. they have made many friends. They have met many obstacles which they needed to personally overcome. They each have their own set of success stories to tell about the past two years.

Richard is a pharmacist. After I married him, his job transferred him to Kansas City, Missouri. I moved with him and let the boys stay in the two-bedroom apartment in family housing. They are surviving the apartment scene very well. They are learning about paying bills on time, shopping for groceries and cooking their own dinners. They wash their own laundry. They maintain their own schedules and face their own consequences when they miss an important appointment. Under the protection of university housing, they are learning how to live independently.

Although I am in constant communication with them and remind them that I am still their mother and still *in charge,* I know they are both preparing very well to step into society.

The fact that both Russell and Bobby have done well in school and have both accomplished many amazing achievements makes me proud of my two sons. However, the fact that I am most honored by is that both of my sons love life. They love to learn and are happy about discovering new talents. They are kind to people and are very diplomatic. They are not perfect nor do they have perfect lives. But they work hard at what they do, and when they finally do step out into society, I know that they will continue to honor me with their integrity, human compassion and love of life.

As I said at the beginning of this book, I made countless mistakes during my tenure as a homeschooling single mother. But as I look at what my two sons have accomplished and consider the possibilities that are ahead for each of them, I am glad I did what I did. I'm sure I would do it again.

BIBLIOGRAPHY

Doman, Glenn J. *How to Teach Your Baby To Read.* New York: Random House, 1964

Parents. New York, NY: Gruner + Jahr USA Publishing, published monthly.

Benson, Reed. "Private Schools: A Seedbed For Greatness." Diss. Malto, ID: National Center For Constitutional Studies, 1981

Hi-Ho Cherri-o is a registered trademark of Parker Brothers a Division of Tonka Corp. Beverly, MA. 01915

Grunwald, Lisa, and Joew McNally. "The Amazing Minds Of Infants." *Life* 16 (July 1993): p46 (9)

Moore, Raymond S. and Dorothy Moore. *School Can Wait.* Provo, Utah: Brigham Young University Press, 1979

Typical Course of Study. Chicago, IL: World Book, Inc., a Scott Fetzer company

Kesye, Ken. *One Flew Over The Cuckoo's Nest.* New York: Penguin Books, 1963

48 Hours with Dan Rather. New York, NY: Columbia Broadcasting System.

Animaniacs. Los Angeles, CA: Warner Bros.

ORDER FORM

If you would like additional copies of *About Face: A Redirection in Education,* fill out the order form below. Please print and use black or blue ink. Allow 2 to 3 weeks for delivery. Please do not send cash!

☐ Money Order
☐ Credit Card - *Circle one* (Mastercard, Visa, Discover, Novus only)

Card #____________________________ Exp. Date: ___________

Name ____

Address ____

Phone(s) ____

Please send _____ copies @ ~~$9.95 per copy~~ $7.95 $_______

Shipping and handling (domestic only, ~~$3.50 per~~ $1.50 book) $_______

Sales tax, Missouri residents please add 6.98% per book $_______

TOTAL PAYMENT $_______

Credit Card orders may call (816) 318-~~1110~~ 1289
or fax orders to (816) 318-~~1119~~ 1289

For mail requests using money orders send to:
About Face
P.O. Box 1293
Raymore, MO 64083

For lecture or seminar information,
contact Eva Seibert at (816) 318-~~1110~~ 1289